Sergio Beva

Brain Mechanics

It's a little the working prototype
of an artificial vision system
similar to that of humans,
a little like a model of the human brain.

1

Brain Mechanics

It's a little the working prototype of an artificial vision system similar to that of humans, a little like a model of the human brain.

Author Sergio Beva

Published by Sergio Beva
Printed in 2021
ISBN 978 – 1 – 008 – 99885 -8

Contacts
info@beva.it
www.beva.it

To be creative we need to be somewhat underemployed in order to give free rein to our thoughts.

To my parents, to whom I owe great liberty.

Preface

The phrases which introduce this book are those of James Watson, co-discoverer of DNA, and Silvio Ceccato, a whimsical man of thought who brought cybernetics to Italy. The first describes my way of life, which has been possible thanks to my parents, to whom this book is dedicated. It aims to be a modest step towards the ambitious purpose of understanding the functioning of the brain or, at least, its rational activities, through mechanization. The first person to recognize that the brain is the centre of the activity of thought in humans and animals was Alcmaeon of Croton. We have only uncertain information about him, including his date of birth. Aristotle said that Alcmaeon was young when Pythagoras was already old. It seems that he dissected animals and saw the nerves that led from the eyes, ears and tongue to the brain. Before him, but also for centuries after, because he did not convince everybody, the seat of cognitive activities was believed to be in the heart and the brain was considered to be an irrelevant organ: the Egyptians didn't conserve the brains of mummies and Aristotle himself thought it served to cool the blood. Like every other science, the study of the brain flowered above all in the last century, thanks to discoveries in microscopy, in chemistry and the revelation of the electric current in a scientific branch called physiology. Then there were the psychologists who studied human and animal behaviour in relation to the brain. Immediately after the Second World War, above all in the United States of America, it was thought that the brain could be simulated with electric calculators, which had just been successfully constructed. The calculators kindled the enthusiasm of many who came to likening them to the brain and calling them electronic brains. The study of the brain and the attempts to simulate its behaviour went on with great intensity. I leave it to the reader to judge if the progress in artificial intelligence is due to conceptual discoveries or rather to the increased power of the calculators. Whether useful or in vain, there has been a great deal of financing in this direction. The latest (2013) which in ten years will provide 1,300,000,000 euros, are two enormous projects, the first is the European Community 'Human brain' project and the second is the USA 'BRAIN' initiative. I have always studied alone, I am a self-taught person and I started to be interested in the function of the brain when I was 19 years old. I did it for purely intellectual interest; what was once called 'for the love of science' and, as I was interested in continuing these studies in absolute freedom, I always paid for them, including the necessary instruments. I don't want to bore the reader with my personal history, which is that of an absolutely ordinary man. At the base of my work is the idea that the brain is an apparatus that permits living beings to navigate their way in their surroundings, anticipating the development of situations in order to profit from them or avoid damage. This is in agreement with the evolutionary theories of Darwin and Wallace. My work is also influenced by the thoughts of Democritus and heavily by those of David Hume. It is linked to the brain and its function through neurophysiology and psychophysics. The model of the brain that I have developed aims to be, as much as is possible, 'human like'. As far as it has been possible for me, and this has happened through visual perception, I have constantly verified the theories I was formulating with programs that function on any type of PC. I agree with Richard Feynmann when he says: what I can't do I'll never understand. As in this text theories on language also appear, I give warning that these have not been experimented. This is not a book on philosophy or psychology, it is substantially a book on physics. In fact a parallel can be traced between the study of the atom and that of the brain: In the first years of the 20th century the physicists perfected the idea of the atom, that the chemists of the 19th century had foreseen, based on experiments with radiations from matter emitted when it was heated. Nobody had ever seen an atom and, as in the physics of the extremely small, even now our ideas are not clear and, in my opinion, never will be. In a similar way as the atom, also the brain can be understood through the manifestation of its activity with psychological tests and with neurophysiological experiments. Unlike the atom, I think that the brain can be understood because its components, neurons, synapses,... are not part of of the microcosm like atomic and subatomic matter. On the contrary the brain can be mapped, in fact we already possess a detailed map of the modest brain of a worm, consisting of a thousand neurons, without, however, succeeding in understanding how it works. My study begins with the perception (I use this word even though it doesn't define well) of how animals manage to survive and get around in their environment without possessing a structural language and therefore it is with the perception that the brain carries out this task. Structured language is an ulterior construction, a faculty of humans, that allows them to improve the predictive activity of the brain but always based on perception. Since, at least in man, vision is the most important sense, in order to understand the human brain, it is necessary, first of all, to understand how the visual system works. Reflecting on evolution it seems to have, in humans and in superior animals, two different functions: The first is that which permits spatial orientation and the second is for recognising objects. If we consider a fly, its eyes seem to have only the first function; food is recognised by the sense of smell or better, the chemiosensorial apparatus. In low-level vertebrates a vast area of the brain is dedicated to the chemiosensorial apparatus and they recognise objects above all from their smell and taste. In humans it is no longer like this: smells and tastes have a marginal importance when recognising objects. I have dedicated myself above all to this second function of the visual apparatus and will set it out in this book. However, I have my own ideas about the other function and will say something marginal about it. Always in the margins I will touch on the mind and consciousness. I wonder if these words make sense and what is their relation to the function of the brain. From this point of view, using language which is not usual for me, I can say that sight is a conscious activity while recognition is an unconscious activity.

Note.

The image on the cover is a photograph of a bust of Democritus, also thought to be of Eraclitus. It was taken from the Italian Wikipedia site.

THE IMAGE IN THIS BOOK, SOMETIMES IN COLOUR, ARE ALSO ON THE SITE www.beva.it which accommodates also the corrections and discussions with readers, which I invite to contact me at the email address: info@beva.it

Chapter I – The World and the Brain

Preliminary remarks

In this chapter I will explain my conception of the physical universe and the brain. It is a chapter on philosophy in which I lay out also the choices and the priorities in my work. They are my opinions and it is not possible to verify if they are true, as it is for every philosophical theory, but they have guided me and still guide me in the projection and construction of an artificial brain whose function, on the contrary, can be verified.

1. A mechanistic model of the brain is needed in a universe that (probably) is not mechanistic.

The brain is connected to the world through the senses. Limiting myself to the human visual system I must ask myself what happens in the brain when I look out of the window and see the mountain with its red rocks, its green woods and the blue sky above. Paradoxically the study of neurophysiology seems to generate further confusion. In fact every image is turned upside down on the retina, it goes on the receptors, cones and rods, which converge in different ways on each single fibre of the optic nerve. Then there are cells that connect them horizontally. I would like to point out that the receptors, that react to the light, are situated under the horizontal cells, amacrine and ganglion, and are not exposed to the light but covered! This observation alone is enough to demonstrate to us how complexity and confusion reign in the visual apparatus and alerts us to the great effort that will be necessary for anyone who wishes to make clear its function. The nerves of the two eyes then meet in the chiasma and then reach the two opposing geniculate bodies (but a portion remains in the same cerebral hemisphere) and go on to the optical cortex. Not to mention the fibres that proceed from the optic nerve to the mid-brain and then from here also go to the optical cortex. During this passage from the eye to the brain the visual information is elaborated (less in man but always more going down the evolutionary scale). It makes sense to me to accentuate the optical cortex: vision occurs in this area. Humans, but also the superior animals who are deprived of this are blind. This does not happen with inferior animals, for example mice without an optical cortex orient themselves in their environment more or less as before this loss. Evidently the role of mid-brain vision is still important for them, while it is almost extinct in humans. I say 'almost extinct' in humans because in my opinion, blind vision, which was discovered in 1973 by Poppel, Held and Frost in cases where the human optical cortex was completely destroyed, is exactly this. Given this, in the cortex, the image on the retina generates disproportionate stimulations and splits into scattered fragments with a form that is in no way similar to the image projected onto the retina and which we can see. Where is the image of my mountain with its rocks, its woods and the blue sky above? Not on the optical cortex and in no other part of the brain. If we say that what we see is on the optical cortex, it does not mean that the stimulation of its cells reconstructs the image on the retina. Those who are used to mathematics would say it is not a bad thing: the points on the retina are in correspondence with the points on the optical cortex; some would call this topographic. Therefore it is easy to go back from these to retinal stimulation, that is the reconstruction of the form projected on the retina. The problem is that this correspondence is not precise; in fact it is not certain that a nerve that comes from the retina arrives at a cell on the optical cortex. The topographic correspondence needs to be considered but this alone would lead to the reconstruction of a blurred and confused image. Rather I consider that what we see is the representation of the information brought by the nerves of the retina, which is already partially elaborated and mostly elaborated by the cortex itself. Everybody knows that a fly's brain is different from that of a human. Both the human and the fly have two eyes which receive information from the outside world but it is impossible that these two beings have the same vision of the world. The eyes of the fly, already quite different from those of humans, perceive little more than variations of light. However, both for the human and for the fly, what they see is the world. One could say: man is superior to a fly, the world is how humans see it and not how it is seen by these inferior animals. In this way, in my opinion, we fall into an error: anthropocentrism, not different from geocentrism. Who knows what the world is really like, what we see is a mass of information which allows us to foresee the development of situations, relative to our elementary needs, which are satisfied in the environment in which the eye and the brain were formed. We see the trees and the houses but the fly doesn't. Who knows how a hypothetical being, different from us and coming from another planet, would see them, or even only a frog, which has a visual system different from humans or flies. The trees and the houses represent necessary things, who knows what is the reality. Already Democritus 2500 years ago in his 'Book of Shapes' writes that we know nothing that corresponds to the truth of what is around us, a sort of configuration forms in us. However he believed that behind the perceptual illusion there was a reality of atoms that move in the void. About 2000 years later David Hume goes beyond this mechanistic conception, which confuses the world with a mechanistic model of the world and claims that the nature of the world outside the brain is unknown, that what we call physical reality is a mental representation and physical laws are nothing more that recurrent behaviour in this representation. How is this mental representation formed or, in other words, this model? If we look at evolution we see in it enormous suffering and massacres aimed at eliminating the unfit. We are the lucky children of this fight and our bodies, including the brain were formed by a series of events in which we see no philosophic intent aimed at the knowledge of being and its essence. Were we born not to live as brutes but to follow virtue and knowledge? For heaven's sake! This is an unconditional opinion, without confimation, of the Supreme Poet Dante. Rather the necessity to have an organ, the brain, that can foresee the development of situations in order to benefit from them or avoid damage, is what comes from my observations. It is, or rather, it has taken form, together with the senses that connect it to the environment in which humans live, to satisfy the needs of the living. Transferred to a different setting, the brain will not give the right predictions because neither it nor the senses will be able to grasp the warning signs. The physics of the extremely small is the proof of what I say: the extension of the laws obtained from the macrocosm lead to the theories that are less and less predictive when the studied bodies become smaller and smaller. The results that come from observing the extremely fast are incredible: distance and time, based on all our experiences in the physical world, are different if measured between two subjects in relative fast motion. Personally I doubt that physics can make more progress in this area and it is from the twenties of the last century that each discovery in atomic and subatomic physics only came about thanks to the increased potency of the machines used to observe the world and these discoveries cannot be connected to a theory with predictive power. On the contrary, it is the discoveries that modify the theories and extend them. Only the mechanistic models, both the atomistic ones of Leucippus and Democritus and the pneumatic ones of the Stoics, have brought serious results to physics, or rather in the knowledge of nature. And that is why, since I was nineteen, by now a long time ago, I keep calling my studies 'Brain Mechanics'. I would like to make it explicit that my research is based on a mechanistic model of the brain, mathematical and deterministic. In fact the mechanistic model is suitable for understanding and describing the biological brain because there are no quantic aspects in its workings: the neurons are composed of a large number of atoms and the electric current between them involves a large number of electrons: we are in the macrocosm, in the area of classical physics, therefore it will be possible to understand the brain in the future, whereas, in my opinion and for the reasons I will elaborate more later, this is not possible for atomic and subatomic physics, never. Having assumed this position, a problem arises: a mechanistic brain cannot make predictions from a world that is probably not mechanistic, given the failures of atomic and subatomic physics. Let us consider a person who we will call Tizio, who observes the world. Tizio's senses, in contact with the world, provoke changes in the state of his brain: In a mechanistic

13

world the brain states, for which we use the first letters of the alphabet: A,B,C,D... are perfectly quantifiable and definable. In other words, if the brain were composed of gears and levers, it would have a precise and specific position, which would define its state; the brain is made of organic material but there is no conceptual change,, we are always in the macrocosm. I use the last letters of the alphabet ...W,X,Y,Z. To note the environmental conditions. The states of the brain are provoked by environmental states and I can know with precision the cerebral state A, because the brain is mechanistic by definition, but not the environmental state X which provokes A: I must define X through the cerebral state, which is completely impossible. It is enough to think that when Tizio hears a sound, his brain assumes a certain state but the same sound can be produced by many different things where 'different things' represents different environmental states which produce the same sound. In this way a real apple and a fake apple seem the same to the eye and produce the same cerebral state. Even with the help of all the senses there is no precision in the definition of the environmental state from the cerebral state: the same cerebral state that produces a good apple can produce another that is the same to the eye , to the senses of smell and taste but poisoned with a poison that tasteless and has no smell or colour. In other words, the cerebral state A can be provoked by many environmental states with very different developments. To get round these weighty considerations it is necessary to reflect on the role that the brain has in the life of animals and humans, even if this makes it necessary to clarify what the word 'life' means.

A being lives when it grows and multiplies, taking what it needs from the environment for this purpose and the brain is the instrument that enables life and serves for

1. predicting the development of situations,

2. carrying out strategies related to these previsions.

A definition of intelligence that is by no means new. A broth that is always the same in space and time, if nutritious, enables life for bacteria but that bacteria does not need a brain. Instead if the broth offers different states which alternate, some beneficial, some poisonous, either the bacteria modifies itself enabling its membrane to recognise the various states and reacting to keep itself out of the poisonous fluids, or the bacteria dies. The cerebral activity is already present in this bacteria and can be found in its external membrane. Such extremely elementary 'brains' develop in relation to the broth in which the microbe lives and its need to filter it. I would not like to evoke a war between the ghosts of Darwin and Lamark. I won't go into the matter of deciding if evolution is a result of adaptation or natural selection. I only say that this behaviour can be interpreted as brain activity because it exploits the advantages and avoids damage. Leaving aside that it doesn't die, the being undergoes evolution and becomes able to live despite more and more complex changes in the environment. The organ adapted for prevision becomes able to pick up emanations (molecules, temperature, vibrations, photons.....) from a complex environment and put into effect strategies for survival as did the original membrane. Evolution has chosen to concentrate predictive activity in a particular organ, the brain, and to connect this with the world through the senses. However, the predictive activity is limited to the environment and the primary needs of the living being. Furthermore the proceeding example of food that is poisoned with a poison that is tasteless and with no colour or smell reveals the partiality of the connection between the senses and the world, from which it is clear that our knowledge of this is incomplete. We cannot know what the world is like and how it works; we can foresee what we need to live with a certain percentage of exactness, in fact we are still here. For now.

If I observe an inferior animal, for example an amoeba, when it envelopes a particle in order to absorb it, first it must understand if this particle is food. I can say that evolution has formed its outline of senses and brain in order that the cerebral state A is established in a certain combination of environmental states X, few or many, whatever they are, able to implement the environmental states Y, that is, the well-being of the amoeba. The brain of the amoeba, faced with the nutrient acquires the state A, which provokes the state B, that is, it absorbs the nutrient. If the amoeba prospers, it has been able to recognize the state X which anticipates the environmental state Y, therefore its brain has functioned well, otherwise the amoeba could die of poisoning. In that case the environmental state X would have erroneously recalled the cerebral state A and then the state B which allows the amoeba to absorb the nutrient. Identically an apple generates in a child the cerebral state A in which the child recognises the apple and this induces in him the cerebral state B which leads him to eat it. However, after eating that which he recognised as an apple, the child will be fortified or poisoned. In the second case, the recognition was not correct, the physical state recognised as an apple has produced the cerebral state B and this has induced the action of eating but without the hoped for result. A cause and effect relationship can be seen between the cerebral states A and B. With an acceptation very different from what is usual, because the cerebral state A which will produce the cerebral state B which brings the child to eat, must be recalled from the environmental states X (good food) which produces the environmental states Y (the well-being of the child). It can be that the cerebral state A is produced by poisoned food.

Within the cerebral states there is the relation but it is wrong. (in absolute terms) to extend this idea also in the physical world: It would confuse the cerebral state A with the X states which generate them, not without error, in certain environments and, anyway, based on a certain purpose. Let's suppose, for example, that an animal is immune to a poison which infects a fruit. Its brain can give the same state A=all fruit together for X. If, however, the animal is not immune to the poison, it must learn to distinguish within X two subsets, each of which generates a cerebral state A=good fruit and B=poisonous fruit. The cause and effect relationship for the first and the second are different.

If we wish to construct an artificial brain, given that we do not know how is the world, we cannot project a sensorial apparatus that connects to something if we do not know what this something is, and find in it the signs of a certain purpose. It is not possible to project anything rationally, only by trial and error. Indeed this work has been done by evolution, exterminating all those who could not adapt. However, the situation is not so desperate for us, anybody who wishes to build an artificial brain has the possibility (but it is the only possibility) of copying the work done by nature, even only for the sense of sight. Obviously such a brain could generate previsions only in the environment in which man has grown and for the purposes for which the human brain has developed. My pessimism that the possibility that the physics of microcosm can progress arises from here. Fortunately, the brain does not have quantistic aspects, it is only complicated, messed up with the residue of partially or totally abandoned evolutionary paths, sometimes superimposed by more effective systems. In the study of the brain and its capacity to foresee, in order to follow the path of evolution, I should have started by taking interest in the chemiosensorial system, which is very important in inferior animals, instead I concentrated on vision and not even that of the mid-brain, which is also found in inferior animals, but on human sight, limited to the recognition of shapes, not to the simpler capacity of the visual system related to movement in the world: I have noted that recognition comes about above all through the angles of shapes.

Chapter II – Connections

Preliminary Notes

In this chapter I will present elements of various disciplines for which it is essential to have a clear and present understanding in order to understand the rest of the book. Those who already know these arguments can move on.

1. Elements of neurophysiology and bases of the model for interpreting the human visual system.

The retina is composed of receptors, cones and rods which emit electrical impulses of a certain frequency. This frequency increases when struck by light but also remains in the dark, even if very low. I will not go into the description of equipment for detecting these electrical impulses but only add that the frequency is the number of impulses in each second. There are three kinds of cones, each of which is sensitive to a certain spectrum of electromagnetic frequencies: These spectrums are large, that is, they have many frequencies and they superimpose each other. One can say that the cones are responsible for seeing colours. Their role in seeing colours is neither direct nor immediate. The rods and cones are not distributed uniformly on the retina: the former are abundant in the peripheral parts, the latter in the central part. The rods are united in tufts, each of which converges on a fibre of the optic nerve. Instead, in the cones there is less convergence, sometimes only one cone connects to a fibre of the optic nerve. The connection between these receptors and the fibre of the optic nerve is not direct, it passes through other cells which also establish other parallel connections. Amongst them the ganglion cells are of particular interest. They have been distinguished by Enroth-Cugell and Robson in cells X, Y and W. The X cells have a tonic response, that is "roughly" directly proportional to the light and they are more abundant in the central part of the retina. The Y cells have a phasic response, that is, they respond brusquely to variations of light and are chiefly in the peripheral part of the retina. The W cells instead, are distributed uniformly and respond to specific stimulations from the environment. The optic nerves which come from the X cells go to the striated area of the visual cortex by way of the lateral geniculate body (fig. 1). Some optic nerves which come from the Y and W cells follow the same route, others instead go to the upper colliculus and then go on to areas of the visual cortex that are not striated. In my opinion the Y cells are attentional devices since they snap into action according to the environmental condition. The W cells are a residue of evolution as they carry out an elaboration of other signals already on the retina and it is known that this is increasingly marked the more the evolutionary scale descends. There is a correspondence (called topographic) between every point on the retina and every point on the striated area (also called area 17) of the visual cortex. However, the proportions are not respected. In fact a small proportion of the retina near the fovea, stimulates a vast part of area 17. This is probably due to a different convergence of the receptors on the optic nerve.

In 1962 Hubel and Wiesel discovered that the brain is sensitive to angles. In fact these neurophysiologists, exploring the visual cortex of cats, observed cells that responded exclusively when the cat was shown bars inclined in a certain way. Entering in the grey matter is was possible to observe a column of nerves that all responded in the same direction.

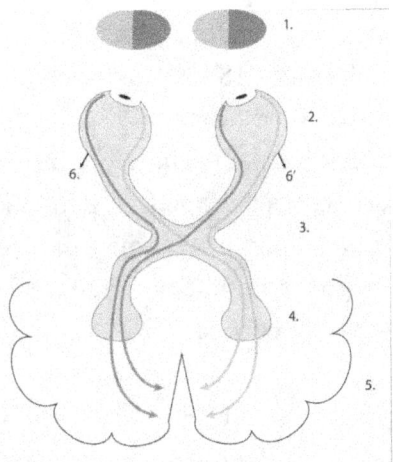

Fig.1 1. The observed object - 2. Retina - 3. Chiasm - 4. Lateral geniculate body, 5 Visual cortex - 6 and 6'. Nerves which go to the upper colliculus.

These columns could be considered clustered in structures called hypercolumns, in which there were columns able to pick up each inclination with minimal margins of 10-15 degrees. Subsequent studies have led to understanding that in the columns there are three types of cells that, entering the brain, are in the order: simple cells, complex cells and hypercomplex cells. The first are sensitive to inclination, the second to inclination and the direction of movement, the third respond to the specific features of the object. Personally I think that the third is a route abandoned by evolution, also because they are in area 17. The complex and hypercomplex cells are sensitive to angles but little interested in the position of the image on the retina. Their stimulation remains if the image (an inclined bar) is moved within a certain area of the retina. Recent studies pose questions about the properties of the hypercomplex cells as described by Hubel and Wiesel: I won't go into this because the new discoveries are not connected to this text. Their importance is that most of them are in the areas 18 and 19 which are associative areas where the nerves which come from the W cells by way of the collicutus-thalamus are abundant. Therefore the interpretive models that I will propose are only about the first two kinds of cells. Substantially I will discuss in this text only the "principal optical pathway", that which goes from the retina to the lateral geniculate body and then to the visual cortex.

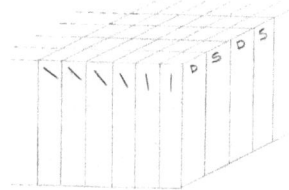

Fig.2

Another structure is found in the hypercolumn: column planes that respond to an eye alternating with planes that respond to the other eye as in fig.2; but also cells that respond to colour and have little sensitivity to inclinations.

To these discoveries must be added the preceding one of the philosopher Mach, who noticed a very white line on the light grey side and a very black line on the dark grey side of an image of contrast between white and black. (fig.3). It wouldn't change anything if instead of the greys there were white and black, provided that the passage between the two colours was shaded. This would have no sense from a physical point of view: those lines were not on the image. The luminance, that is, the reflected light of the image; a physical phenomenon, has lost the proportion with the brilliance, a psychological phenomenon, that is, with the value that the sense of sight has given to the light. Today this fact is explained by neurologists with the presence of inhibiting or stimulating zones in the retina, in the geniculate body and in area 17. However, while in the retina and the lateral geniculate body these zones have a circular symmetry, in area 17 they form stimulating or inhibiting stripes (neurologists claim this with some certainty). It is noted at the level of the visual cortex that the signal of a cell is inhibited when it is placed in the visual field of a bar perpendicular to that which stimulates it. Perhaps the very form of stimulating or inhibiting stripes is responsible for this fact. In any case also lateral inhibition becomes a phenomenon tied to angles. It has been supposed that nature transmits information through two channels: one which carries the very approximate information of luminosity and another channel which carries information of contrasts.

Fig. 3

This supposition is comfirmed by the fact that in the brain there are two distinct areas: one that receives the information of contrasts from which it derives the inclination of outlines and the other, of more antique origin, that responds to the intensity of light and its frequency (colour) very approximately. Going up the evolutionary scale, one notes the increase of antagonistic cells, which probably reveal contrasts.

In conclusion, beyond the role of Y cells, which I will specify later, I have decided to base the recognition of forms on three fundamental aspects of the visual system:

1. Lateral inhibition which permits the observation of the contours of a shape, but not only that;
2. the response of the cells of the visual area to angles,
3. the convergence of signals, which is already manifest on the retina, where more receptors go to the same fibre of the optic nerve.

In addition there is evidence of directional inhibition.

2. Mathematical Elements

A variable z is said to be the function of two variables x and y when set the values to a pair of x and y carrying out the opportune arithmetical operations, obtains a value of z, written as

$$z=f(x,y) \quad (1)$$

or similar notations. For example $z=2x+y^2$ is a particular case of the function of type (1) because two random values are attributed to the pair x, y, for example x=3 and y=2. Carrying out the arithmetical calculations one has $z=2*3+2^2$, that is z=10. Using geometrical representation of this function through a cartesian coordinate system helps intuition a lot. Think of a geographical map in relief, a small area of territory in which no big mistakes are made in no considering the roundness of the Earth. If the map is framed, choose the top of the frame as the origin of the Cartesian axes. Understanding the function that describes it means that the values of x and y correspond to the values of z, which measure geometrically the height of the reliefs in the points x,y. Every point of the plane x,y corresponds to a certain height z, that of the relief on the map. From a certain point of view there is no difference, therefore, between the type (1) function, called analytic and the map in relief. Given the values of x and y, the value of z can be obtained in both cases. In the first case arithmetic is used for the calculations, in the second, measurements are taken with a ruler.

Lines of different levels (contour line) can be traced on this map in relief, for example all the adjacent points that are 3cm from the base can be joined, then those at 4cm, 6cm etc...

Having said this, if I consider a point P on the side of a real mountain, for example, a sloping field, I can ask, "where is the maximum inclination?", which is like asking "if I pour a bucket of water on P, in what direction will the water flow in order to go down?" A mathematical operation which resolves this problem is the gradient. Since I elaborate data on a calculator, I will use a numerical method which will resolve the problem of finding which is the angle of maximum inclination of the surface on each one of its points and also what is the value of the inclination. In fact it is not enough to say where the water of the example will go but also if it precipitates or almost stagnates because the ground is almost level. The mathematical entity which supplies information on the inclination is the gradient. It is a vector which, as such, has three features: 1) the magnitude, which represents (in this case) how is steep the slope, 2) the direction, which represents the line where the water flows and 3) the versus, which specifies the direction, in this case it is down. Each direction has got two versus, in this case up and down.

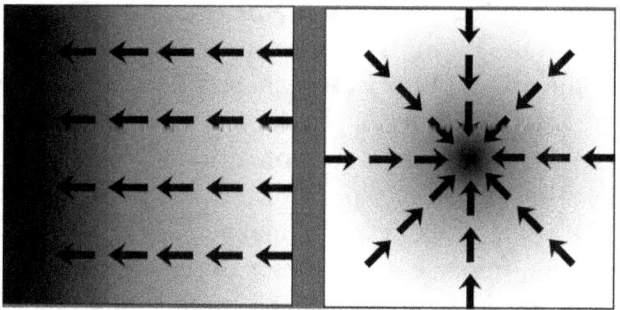

Fig.4

In fig.4 the gradient is represented by arrows on the two surfaces: think that the black part is the highest point of a cone in the image on the left and the highest point of an inclined plane in the image on the right. The spilt water would go down in the direction of the arrows but in the opposite versus.

Please note that the tangent to the contour line and the gradient are orthogonal.

Two vectors can be summed with the rule of the parallelogram studied at school and a vector **a** can also be decomposed along the direction of the straight lines r and s fig.5. The foot of the vector **a** is brought to the point of intersection O of the straight lines r and s. Then from the tip of **a**, a parallel of s is traced until it meets r in the point R. In the same way, from the tip of **a**, a parallel of r is traced until meets s in the point S. The two resulting vectors OR and OS are called components of **a** along the directions r and s.

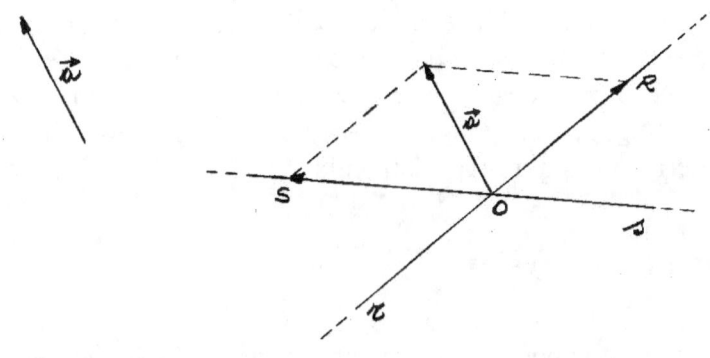

Fig.5

In mathematics and in physics one speaks of field when a quantity has a value in every point of an area of space. One speaks of the field of temperature because in every point of the space the value of the temperature can be defined: one speaks of the field of the velocity of water in a river because in every point of the river, the water has its velocity. Temperature is a scalar quantity, that is it has no direction, but only module, while velocity is a vector, in the case of temperature one speaks of a scalar field and in the case of velocity, a vector field. If the fields are superimposed, they can be summed together, if they are scalar, with the the rules of sum of arithmetic, if they are vectors, with the rule of the parallelogram.

Instead of speaking of a topological transformation of an image, in the case of homeomorphism, I prefer to imagine an image designed on a sheet of rubber and then say that the topological transformations are those obtained by stretching the sheet (only a little!); in fact it doesn't seem to me that the visual system, even that of a small child, accepts such extreme transformations such as topological ones that change a rectangle into a circle. There are limits that I will place on the deformations through the operative definition of the concept of similarity, as understood by a child: a child would never find that a rectangle and a circle are similar. I speak of the topological recognition of forms, despite being aware that the name is not perfectly fitting, because Piaget, a Swiss psychologist, used it before me to describe the sight of a small child.

3. Elements of physics

I call to mind some photometric quantities, which I will define approximately. I will use the units of measurement of the international system. The fundamental photometric unit in the IS system is the candle (cd). Its current definition, set by the International Office of Weights and Measures in Paris is incomprehensible to the educated reader not specialised in physics. Having said this, the luminous intensity of 1 candle in the international system comes close (roughly!) to the intensity of light emitted by a normal wax candle. Consider the source of a point of light having the intensity of 1cd; one can imagine the flame of a wax candle if one wishes, it radiates a sphere of luminous flux around itself. Putting a sheet of paper of $1m^2$ at a distance of 1m from this, obviously perpendicular to the rays, the illumination produced will be of 1 lux. If the sheet of paper is moved further away from the candle, Its illumination diminishes, obviously it diminishes also if the sheet of paper is inclined.

A surface of of 1 m² that shines with its own light or reflected (therefore also illuminated like the Moon, a river...) that gives out a light of the intensity of 1cd has the luminance of 1 nit. One can speak of the luminance of the lunar surface or luminance of the solar surface but for our purposes it concerns environmental luminance, for example, the page of a book and the illuminance that this produces on the retina of the observer. It is not inappropriate to give an example to clarify the difference between illuminance and luminance. Two sheets of paper, one white, one black are placed near to each other in the same sunlight. Both enjoy the same illuminance but their luminance is different because the white sheet of paper reflects more light than the black.

Illuminance produced (in lux)

from the night sky	0.0003
from the full Moon	0.2
from artificial light in the open	10-100
from artificial light indoors	100-1000
from the Sun	5000-80000

Luminance (in nit)

Full Moon	2500
Flames	10,000-20,000
White paper in full sunlight	30,000
The Sun	1,600,000

The illuminance of a body is a quantity tied to the light that arrives on that body. The luminance is tied to the light emitted by that body whether reflected light or its own light. Some values of illuminance and luminance are quoted in the two preceding tables.

There are motions that repeat themselves at regular intervals, always the same, like heart beats or the breaking of waves on the beach. These motions are called periodic. In physics frequency is the number of times a periodic motion repeats in one second. Frequency is measured in herz (hz). For example, if a wheel turns three times in a second, it has a frequency of 3hz. If a cell emits 15 electric impulses in one second, it emits with a frequency of 15hz. In electrodynamics the intensity is defined as the charge that passes in a conductor in each unit of time. One can speak of the intensity of the charge that goes through the optic nerve. The concept merges with that of frequency because it is proportional to it, if the electric charge of every neuronal discharge is constant.

Chapter III – The fundamentals of vision

Preliminary remarks

When I was 15 I asked myself how it was possible to see things, how images were formed in the brain. I went to a library and borrowed some books but they did not clarify my ideas. From these readings I remember a beautiful image: according to an Indian sage the world that appears in our brains is like a reflection on a sheet of crystal. Of course it is useless to say that this reflection has not been found on our visual cortex nor in any other part of the brain. However, there are stimulations on the visual cortex that can be related to the stimulation of the retina since they derive from the elaboration of the electrical impulses coming from it. The treatment of the signals coming from the retina is the information that the brain has of the world. It enables us to orientate in the world and recognise its objects. The claim to "see" the image of the world painted by the stimulation of the visual cortex has no sense. I must navigate the world, avoiding holes, dodging obstacles,... and in the brain there is information about the world which allows me to take action. It appears to me as its image. I think this is a conscious activity because it involves a continuous adaptation of the living to the transformations of the world. Instead I think that the work of recognition is subconscious because the object is what it is and is always analysed with the same automatic process, like the work of a gland.

1. Luminance and brilliance

Both the Sun at midday and the full Moon at night allow us to see, in fact it is possible to walk in the mountains and in the fields also in the nights with a full Moon. The illuminance passes from 50,000-80,000 lux during the day to 0.2 lux during the night with a variation of about 300,000 times. It follows that the variation of luminance of the fields, of the roads, of everything to the natural light which reflects the light of the Sun or the Moon is enormous. Therefore also the variation of the illuminance of the retina which receives this reflected light is enormous and remains considerable despite the variation of the area of the pupil, which tends to normalise it. As the discharge of the retinal receptors has a variation of frequency in the order of a thousand herz, I think it has no sense to place this frequency as proportional to the intensity of the retinal illuminance. We must not forget that we are dealing with a biological system, approximate, not with laboratory instruments. In fact,under this hypothesis, the image of an object projected on the retina, brings about a remarkable and highly detectable variation of the frequency of the receptors in the passage between the   sunlight of the day and the nocturnal light of the moon. However in the hypothesis that the discharge of the receptors is proportional to its illuminance, two parts of a sheet of paper, one white, one black, that are projected on the retina, would give place in the underlying receptors to discharges more or less of identical frequency, whether they were under the white part of the image of the sheet of paper or if they were under the black part, because the retinal illuminance produced by them would not be so different in relation to the enormous variation between the light of the Sun and that of the Moon. The black part of the sheet of paper, even if it reflects less light than the white one, still reflects a great amount. This is because the average variation of luminance of the sheet of paper in the Sun or in the lunar light is great, while when the sheet of paper is in the Sun, the variation of luminance between the two parts, white and black, is relatively small. If the frequency of the impulses of the receptors were proportional to their illuminance and so determined the sensation of light and dark, the sheet of paper in question, half white and half black, would appear to be a confused mix of light greys when in the sunlight and dark greys when in artificial light. The black part and the white part would not be well defined in both cases. In my opinion the visual system succeeds in resolving this problem, apart from the variation of the area of the pupil, with an apparatus, conceptually constructable, that regulates the sensitivity of the retinal receptors. In my hypothesis, it should act in a very slightly different way in monochromatic vision compared with chromatic vision. Peripheral vision is substantially monochromatic because in the periphery of the retina there are principally rods, insensitive to light frequency. Instead the central vision is essentially chromatic because in the centre of the retina there are principally cones, sensitive to the frequency of light. In peripheral vision (or anyway in monochromatic) there are two regulations.

1) One which measures the illuminance of the retina and acts on the pupil in order to normalise it. In reality the pupil succeeds only in mitigating the enormous variation of the illuminance.
2) The second regulation is aimed at the purpose of permitting the detection of the edges of figures, that is, to generate a significant difference of discharges of the receptors which are found under the white and black of the image projected on the retina of the previous example.

Mechanizing the first regulation is extremely easy, the only precaution is that it must be fast in order that the receptors are not ruined by the excessive light. In the visual system there are cells which act quickly and I think that this is their purpose. The second

33

regulation can be resolved by hypothesising an apparatus of the visual system, that modulates the discharge of the retinal receptors according to the total illuminance of the retina. Its adaption to the light must be slow. I don't know where this hypothetical human apparatus that acts on the pupil can be found, surely it exists: I will reason that it could be located in the eye and that it proceeds in relation to the measure of illuminance of the the retina and acting on the sensitivity of the receptors in a way that summing up their discharges in all the retina in a unit of time, a constant result is obtained, independently of the illuminance of the retina. In other words, probably because of an inhibiting process, the same impulses leave from all the retina every second, whether a lot or a little light enters the eye. The quantity in question is known in electrodynamics as intensity of the electric current, defined as the number of charges that pass through a conductor in time. In this way the discharge of the receptors loses proportionality with the illuminance of the retina but local variations of the illuminance of the retina bring about variations of the frequency of the underlying receptors, which are not proportional to the illuminance and therefore flattened, but the difference between the average value of the illuminance and the local value is therefore remarkable and highly detectable.

Perhaps it is appropriate to give an arithmetical example. In a particular world, lost in the universe, the luminance varies between 100,000 units of maximum luminance and 0 of minimum; in that world the visual system of the people generates discharges with variations of the frequency 1000 hz and 0. An observer looks at a sheet of paper that is half white and half black. The white part has a luminance of 80,000 units while the black part has a luminance of 76,000 units.

In the first hypothesis, of a frequency of discharges proportional to the luminance, the frequency of the receptors under the white will be

80hz and the one under the black will be 76hz. A variation of 4000 units produces the variation of 4hz.

In the second hypothesis, calibrating the emission on the average value, the maximum luminance of 80,000 this time produces a discharge of 1000hz and that of 76,000 units produces a discharge of 0. In this case the difference of discharge is detectable also in a not very sensitive system like a biological one.

Naturally this is a simplification. The proportion between the frequency of the discharge and luminance is completely lost but the variations of illuminance between the various zones of the retina now generate frequency of discharge considerably different. The aforementioned proportion was lost anyway because of the workings of the pupil. All this can be mechanized and constructed and it seems reasonable to me that there is an apparatus somewhere in the brain or perhaps in the eye itself. Perhaps they are the horizontal and amacrine cells that permit the average illuminance of the retina to be measured through spatial integration, that is, the sum of the impulses emitted by all the receptors, and inhibit more or less the sensitivity of the rods. Indeed it seems to me to be a function that can be linked to inhibition and to some neurons, discovered in the visual system, which change slowly the response to intensity of the light. I think the work of these neurons reveals itself when we enter a cinema, only after a short time are we able to see. The discharge, when the eye functions in peripheral vision, is constant on all the retina but I have good reason to believe that a similar regulation happens also when the eye works in central vision, limited to the part of the retina that is involved. The illuminance on it causes a further regulation, starting from the regulation that has taken place in peripheral vision but finer. We will see later that peripheral and central vision are alternatives, they cannot coexist. I want to point out finally that in the models I propose, the information about environmental luminance is obtained from the sensitivity of the receptors in peripheral vision, in central vision and from the apparatus that regulates the pupil. In superior animals the information about luminance is not so important: the visual system is directed above all at identifying images, defining their edges. It seems that information about luminance arrives at the cerebral cortex through another channel and interests a type of cerebral cells which are not those which respond to angles, less important than the first in recognising forms. According to the model proposed, in absolute dark, even if the sensitivity of the receptors is at maximum, there will be no discharge because no photon strikes the receptors. This conclusion is not human like because in humans the retinal receptors always generate a discharge of low frequency, called dark discharge. I am aware of this difference. However I will try a simulation of the function of the visual system in which I must reduce the elements which I think are not essential in order to not get lost in too many details.

Modulating the sensitivity of the receptors in order to make constant the intensity of the discharge emitted by the whole retina, explains the paradox of Hering, which explains why a pile of coal by day emits more light than a pile of snow at night but continues to appear black by day. During the day the sum of the impulses emitted by the retina is equal to those that it emits at night. However, during the day the coal forms a black area on the lighter retina and the sensors below emit low-frequency pulses. At night the pile of snow forms a white area on the black of the retina and the underlying receptors emit high frequency discharges. It doesn't matter how the pupils dilate. This is another problem. The frequency of the discharges is not proportional to the luminance of the pile of coal or snow, because the pupil dilates more or less and the luminance of the image projected onto the retina remains disconnected from the brilliance of the pile. If a minimum of information of the absolute luminance remains in the brain, this ends up brightening the coal during the day and darkening the snow at night. So it should reveal itself as a secondary effect, minimum, detectable in some optical illusions. Allow me to tell a personal story: once I took my little daughter aged around 8 or 10 years old to visit the Turin Observatory with a group. Amongst other things we were told in a conference that the Moon is black, because it is made of stones of that colour. I didn't notice this but my daughter touched my arm and said, perplexed: "Dad, but the Moon is white". I was wicked and told her to ask the astronomer. The poor man replied with a flood of words without sense. The night sky has a very low luminosity of about 10^{-4}nit, varying according to the hour and the light pollution produced by cities, but it always remains much lower than the 2500 nit of the Moon. The eye adapts to the low luminosity of the sky, the neuronal discharge stabilizes for that luminosity and the Moon is the luminous particular that interests the underlying receptors which will have a high frequency discharge. It is important to obtain the revelation of the local variations through a substantial variation of the discharge. In addition when I speak of central or peripheral vision and their alternation, the intensity of the discharge that comes from the eye must be equal in both cases, therefore the expression that must be constant per unit of time from the whole retina must be revised.

2. Inhibition and edges

The edges of a figure are very important, in fact the figure is often recognised by its "silhouette", see fig. 6. In the visual system the edge of an object is that which is often isolated from movement. Within a figure there are other edges, for example the mouth of the human body, which serve to define recognition better. The edges of figures are also picked up by lateral inhibition, which registers them and is visible in the optical illusion known as Mach bands. The following function explains lateral inhibition (not directional) and generates Mach bands, so it can be associated with what happens at the level of the retina and the lateral geniculate body. In my opinion, the role of lateral inhibition non-directional and directional, is connected to the recognition of forms through angles, in addition to the perception of edges, as is normally said.

Fig. 6

Now let's start work on the second aspect. As I had to prove this theory on a computer, I had to write it in a mathematical form and since this book is addressed to the educated reader who is not a specialist, I will not go through the predictable steps or long explanations that will seem banal to those who understand mathematics. Consider a plane (x,y) on which a white stripe is drawn on the left and a black one on the right as in fig. 7b), which shades in the centre between the two colours. Along the straight line u, parallel to the axis x, the luminance of every point on it is as in the diagram (P,u) in fig. 7c). Let's consider now a circle fig. 7a) and calculate the average luminance M on it. As a first case I consider a circle that has a diameter greater than the extension of the shaded area. Let's imagine that its centre runs along the straight line u of fig.7b) to obtain the diagram (M,u) in fig 7d) in which is drawn the average luminance M of the circle in the u points. At a distance from the shaded area (M,u) will coincide with (P,u), instead the inclined part of M will have a slope that is minor than P. In fact, making the circle run from left to right, the average brightness of the circle starts to decrease as soon as its circumference enters into the shaded area while the centre is still in the white part. The difference between the two diagrams (M,u) and (P,u) form the graph (Q',u) in fig.7 e). If we think that the circle is illuminated uniformly, the stimulation of the central receptors is equal to the average stimulation of the receptors around it and the function P-M has a value of zero. If M<P as happens when P is near the shaded area and on the left of R, P-M is positive. On the contrary, when all the circle is in the black area, P-M has a value of zero, but when the centre of the circle is just a little to the right of S and in the black area but the circle is almost half way in the black area and the remaining part in the grey area: the average of its internal brightness is greater than that of its centre. Up to now I have moved the centre P of the circle on a straight line parallel to the axis x therefore it would be better to write P(x,y), M(x,y), Q(x,y), a more correct three dimensional representation would be obtained which, however, does not change what I have said. I will not point out the question of the function to avoid making the discussion too weighty. If I make a sum of the functions M and P-M adding a real multiplier k, I obtain the function:

$$Q=M+k(P-M) \qquad (2)$$

as shown in the diagram fig.7f) which recalls the trend of the brilliance with a very clear abscissa point R and a very black abscissa S which are the Mach bands. The Q function is what we see? Not entirely, I would say but it is a great step forward for the comprehension of the visual process.

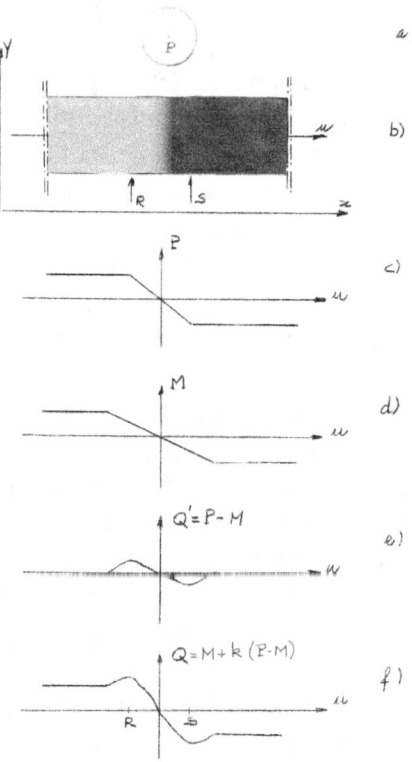

Fig. 7

It is true that the Mach bands do not always appear to sight but only in the case of large shaded areas, more precisely we could say that the diameter of the circle of convergence is less than the extension of the shaded area. In this case the function of Q explains the phenomenon well, it has the same behaviour of brilliance.

We observe Q', fig. 8 e) which presents two distinct extremes connected by a coincident segment with the axis u. In this area, in fact, the slope of P and that of M are equal, differences are found only at the end and beginning of the shaded area. If, instead, the shaded area is narrow, that is, less than the circle of convergence, the direction of Q' is that of fig. 7 e). Consequently the directions of Q are respectively in the fig. 7 f) and 8 f). There does not seem to be a direction of brilliance described by Q in fig. 7 f). In order to be more sure, in fig. 9 I studied the direction of the function Q where the drawing does not have shaded areas but the luminance passes, with a step from a high value to a low value, from white to black. Also in this case Q presents two variations AB and A'B' which are not perceived. For now the function of Q can be considered adherent to the visual perception only in the case of a large shaded area.

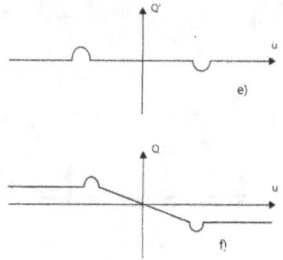

Fig. 8

In the case of the fig. 7 f) and 9 f) Q cannot be considered like brilliance because there is no adherence with experimental facts. I want to present this problem, which will be resolved later. Lastly I would like to say that I have considered the shaded areas with linear and monotonous direction. It maybe that other directions produce

41

other effects which can be the arguments of psychophysical experiments for further verifications of this theory.

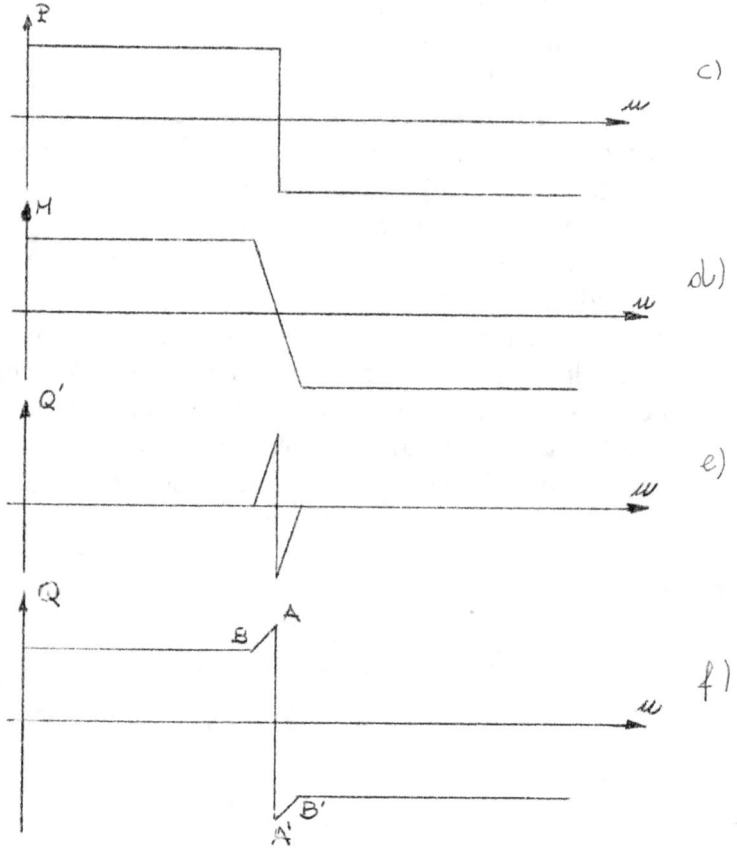

Fig.9

The function of Q is to identify edges? I have already said that not all the points are on the straight line u but on the plane (x,y), therefore the function of P in reality is P(x,y) and its value depends on the point on the plane. It is similar to (1) and the parallel applies with the relief map I have used to explain it. Anyone who has a little experience with the processing of computerized images knows that the figure appears as a table with many numbers, each of which represents the position (x,y) and the brightness $z=P(x,y)$ of an areola. Together these variously illuminated areoles form the image. More technically it can be described as a matrix of pixels. With this data the computer must succeed in distinguishing an object from the background or, and it is the same thing, find the edges of an object in order to establish the distinction between it and the environment in which it is immersed. Initially the threshold was tried, that is, only the points below a certain brightness were tried, assuming that the object was less bright than the environment. These are the small numbers on the table. For this it is enough to order the computer to eliminate the higher numbers up to a given number which is called the threshold and the computer does this. However, the result was a failure, in fact there is no certainty that the object is dark and the background is light. Furthermore, even if this were the case, the computer considers the shadow of the object, which is dark, to be part of the object. Inverting the roles of light and dark and putting mobile thresholds, the results did not improve. This technique was explored in the early days of studies on computerized images, now it is only used for rough industrial applications. I have written the preceding lines to introduce the matter and to make understandable the difficulties that are met carrying out actions that are apparently simple, like distinguishing an object from its background. An educated person, not of this field, who reads these pages must be able to understand them. Whoever wishes to know more can find everything about edge detection (the extraction of outlines) and on segmentation (the isolation of an object from its background) in books on image processing. In order to detect the edges, which means isolating the figure from its background, there is not only the threshold, there are many other methods. In literature the problem is faced using above all gradients and sometimes Laplacians. I tend to adhere to brain function, noting above all that movement isolates the object from its background by activating the phasic Y cells on its edges. I believe that the gradient thus obtained is coarse, a trace to follow and to improve, cultivating the idea of lateral inhibition. In fact children's toys are brightly coloured and attract their attention by moving. Having said this, I believe that the edges of figures are formed slowly in the brain through progressive memorizing and refining. Therefore movement is welcome, strong contrasts are welcome, they are very useful in simplifying the progressive construction of edges inside the brain.

Given this, I propose that there must be an edge where the function $Q'=P-M$ is different from zero. Whoever has tried with a computer will see that in this way a very "thick" edge is extracted. What I want to say is that it shows up as a stripe and not as a line (see fig.12a). In other areas of the image a disturbance called salt and pepper emerges, that is, points where Q' has a different value and marks where there is no edge. These problems are not resolved by filtering Q' with a threshold because in that way there is the risk of eliminating tracts of valid edges. The remedy is to try to simulate the directional inhibition which requires, as a first step, to observe the presence of a gradient of Q between R and S (rif. Fig. 7f). Since I have tested the following theory on the computer, I have preferred to not apply the definition of gradient based on partial derivatives that come from university reminiscences, because they are not suitable for a real surface. The gradients, if they deal with perfect geometrical inclined planes would be parallel as in fig. 4b). In our case it is not so, as it is not so on a mountain side, with holes and rocks. However, as on a mountain side, also in this case, the gradients are generally orientated in the same way, in the direction from high to low. This is on the edges of the figure; instead in the marks, distributed zones which are not edges, the function of Q' is different from zero but its

gradients do not have precise orientation. To capture the gradient I
have considered a circle, fig. 10, much smaller than the matrix of
pixels, which contains the whole image, and I have calculated the
sum of the values of P respectively in the shaded semicircle and the
white one, then I found the difference and I noted it down in the first
column of a table of two columns and in the second I wrote the angle
of AB. Then I rotated AB some degrees and repeated the operation
until I had formed a flat angle. The maximum, in absolute value
(because the direction is not important) of the difference makes it
possible to understand the direction of maximum slope of the
inclined plane and from now on we will call this gradient. In this way
an average of the irregularities of the surface Q is obtained giving the
maximum inclination. I hypothesize that around this detector, when it
indicates a gradient, a vast field of directions spreads out which
influence the other detectors to capture gradients parallel to this.
Think, for example, that a detector has captured a vertical gradient
(rif. Fig.11); the field that it generates causes the other detectors
along the direction AB (which is horizontal) or in its immediate
vicinity to be sensitized to catch the vertical directions of any
stimulated detectors. On the contrary, outside this zone the same field
causes the detectors to inhibit the capacity to catch the vertical
gradients Fig. 11 a. If we consider various optical illusions, I can say
that the field is vast and decreases little moving away from the
detector that has generated it. Furthermore I think that the effect of
sensitizing the detection of the gradient interests a narrow and long
strip straddling AB and for the rest the vertical direction is inhibited.
I think that with psychophysical experiments it is possible to define a
function $f(\rho,\theta)$ quantitatively . Obviously the situation does not
change if the gradient of the detector is not vertical but anyway is
rotated. Incidentally this last observation is not perfectly human like
because neurophysical experiments show that the speed of the

expansion of the lateral inhibition depends on the direction considered.

Fig. 10   Fig. 11

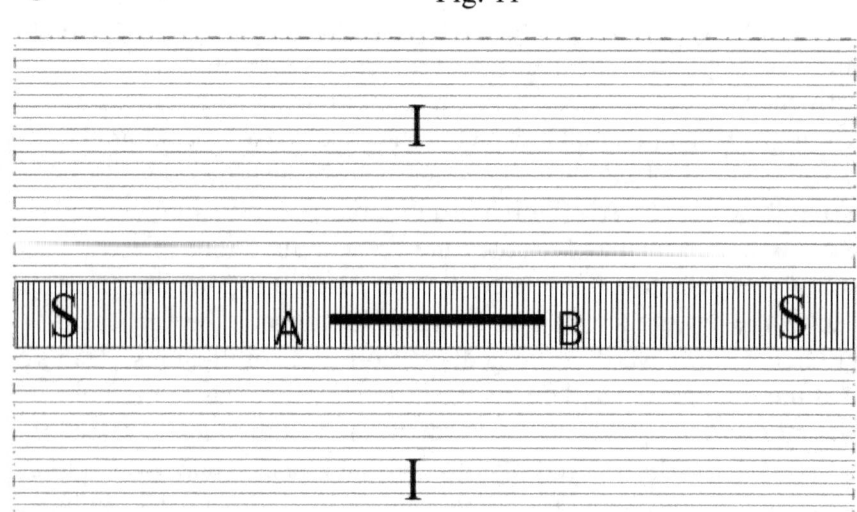

Fig. 11 a). Zone of the inhibitory field generated by the detector which has got AB diameter. S: strip sensitized to detect vertical gradients. I: area inhibited to detect vertical gradients.

I am aware of this, I believe it is impossible to simulate exactly, at least with current knowledge, an apparatus that is so complex and little known like the visual system and I prefer to remain on essential lines. The directional fields sum up, even if it is necessary to remember that they are not vector fields and while for two vectors, being opposites means having opposite orientations, for two directions, being opposite means being perpendicular. However, also with very broad hypotheses on the sum of directions we can say that some gradient detectors, for example, vertical, aligned or with the diameters AB (fig. 10) on the same straight line generate fields that add up, producing a line (or narrow strip) to be defined quantitatively, of an intense horizontal field that magnifies the sensitivity of the underlying detectors to capture vertical gradients. This line, which I will call privileged line or privileged strip (lp) extends also where there are no gradients. Instead outside this strip and therefore around it the field is such as to inhibit the detection of vertical gradients. The directional inhibition agrees with and perfects the non directional inhibition. I have kept them separate because it seems to me that this is the scheme of the visual system and also simulating the former reduces the calculations of the computer.

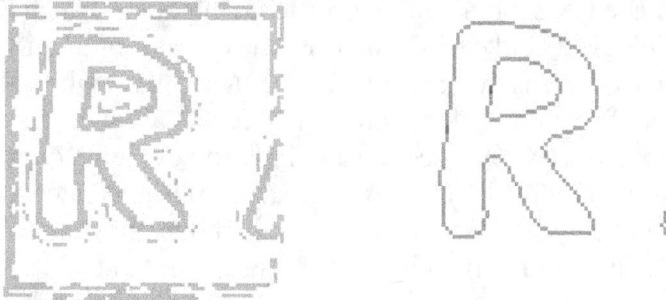

Fig. 12 a)   Fig. 12 b)

The transport of neurophysical evidence on directional inhibition also in this case finds confirmation in the tests carried out on the computer, it produces a thinning of the outline (ref. Fig. 12 b) and explains many optical illusions.

The first psychophysical evidence comes from the close parallel lines that disturb vision and produce strange optical effects because their gradients, lined up one in front of the other, inhibit each other. It is said that the zebra's coat has this design to confound the sight of predators. It also allows us to get closer to the reason why the Mach bands cannot be seen when the Q function comes from a shading that is narrow or nothing, as in fig. 9. In fig. 9 f) one can see a very strong gradient AA' with the consequent formation of privileged direction which eliminates the possibility to observe internal gradients and therefore impedes the observation of gradients on the surfaces AB and A'B', These gradients can be observed on Q in fig. 8 f) from both sides of the maxima which derive from fig.8 e) because they are two lines of maximum, not very intense, that are not able to overpower each other. Q seems to be a good candidate for describing "how much to see". However, it is not rigorously true, further explanations are needed. For the function of Q, tied to non directional inhibition, we have got the parallel with Mach bands that are visible for people; likewise I must find in human vision confirmation for the hypothesis of the privileged direction, tied to directional inhibition which has neurophysiological evidence. To this end the detector of gradients in fig. 13 a) must be considered; set in an imaginary place where there is a gradient of luminosity but there is no directional field. In such conditions of isotropy the direction and intensity of the gradient is obtained. A field in the direction AB in fig. 13 b) is generated above it. Such a field could be produced by a straight line drawn near a detector. The directional field inhibits the sensitivity to the detection of gradients along the normal AB, leaving the sensitivity unchanged along its parallel. We are outside the privileged strip! In other words, the directional component along n is diminished by the presence of the field, while the one along p is unchanged. As a consequence the gradient rotates counter-clockwise, in addition to being decreased in modulus. Let's consider now the angle ABC in fig. 13 c), the side BC is subject to the field that generates the side AB and vice versa, but to fix our ideas let's stay with the first case: every detector on side CB has the component of the normal gradient to AB diminished, therefore the detector rotates counter-clockwise as in fig. 13 a). Each detector on side BC will do it and there will be many small segments M'N', forming a serration on the side. This cannot be seen but it is not an error, the explanation is in the following paragraph. Let's consider now an obtuse angle as in fig, 13 e). The field of dp, produced from the side AB extends around it and affects side BC. Also in this case the loss of sensitivity happens on the normal AB and every gradient detector rotates clockwise (!). Also here serration is found. However, up to now, it is easy to guess there is a connection between these results and the experiments of Carpenter and Blakemore. According to them the acute angle is perceived as expanded and the obtuse diminished. The reader should try to repeat this reasoning inverting the contrasts and considering that the side BC generates the field and AB is subjected to it. Always with regard to serration, a weak contrast could form a "series of steps" as in fig. 13 f) in which the gradient detector eliminates the nearby parallels. Also this is not perceived and we will talk of this in the next paragraph. The hypothesis of dp initiates the explanation of the illusion of Kanizsa in fig. 14. The sides of the triangle are, in fact, the extension of the directional field, in particular of the privileged line, which proceeds from the sides of the white circular sectors cut out of the black circle. Under the lp the gradient detectors are sensitized to detect the normal gradients in it. In this way they tend to pick up and magnify the disturbances (technically speaking the noise) along this direction showing a weak and uncertain contrast which in reality is not there. It remains to explain the effect of depth.

Why does Kanizsa's triangle appear to be in relief? I will try to answer in the following paragraph. What is the use of all this? In my opinion these distortions of the image are the result of the elaboration directed at detecting the angles on the edges of the figure and to isolate it from the background .

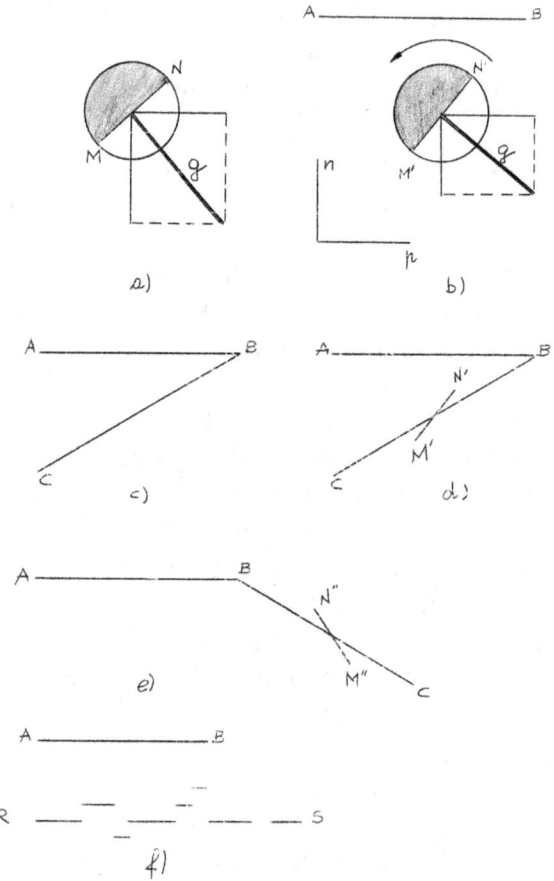

Fig. 13

Fig. 14

3. The isolation of the object from the background

The movement of the object in relation to the background is essential
in order to isolate an object from this. In my opinion, this first part of
the process in humans is certainly operated by the Y cells but I have
not yet experimented my ideas on the vision of movement therefore I
will limit myself to considerations that are valid in the static case.
The visual system when it must isolate an object from the
background, makes use of two strategies:
1. Focusing on an object through the variation of the rays of the
   crystalline lens with the result
   that only the object at the right distance is clear, while the rest
   of the visual scene remains blurred, uncertain;
2. Binocular vision, fig.15. In this the images of the right eye
   and the left eye are different except for the object of interest
   at which both eyes are directed.
I remember that the columns in the visual cortex respond one to the
right eye and one to the left, as is shown in fig. 2, therefore they
transmit the result of the elaboration of the two different images

except for that relative to the object observed by the two eyes which will give "roughly" the same image.

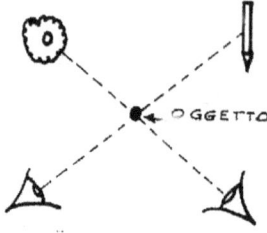

Fig. 15

In other words we will have adjacent columns with dominance on the right which will have different angles from the one with dominance on the left, except for those that derive from the object observed by both eyes, which will have equal angles. It is natural to think of an inhibition between columns that have different angles and a reinforcement between columns that have equal angles, that is those relative to the object. An object, I note, that is already in focus through the work of the crystalline lens while the rest is blurred. As has been said, the edges of a blurred object are more difficult to distinguish than a focused object. Furthermore the gradient on the edges of a blurred object is less intense than the gradients that form on the edges of a focused object. The defined edges materialise both through focus and binocular vision of the same object. This operation causes the generation of edges, even if uncertain, also where they do not exist.

Imagine that we are looking at a ziggurat, a truncated form of pyramid, from a helicopter that is stationary, in perpendicular, above it. In this situation there is the perception of relief (or depth if you prefer) for the smallest level of the ziggurat. If the gaze is concentrated on the upper level, the lower level seems blurred, as they seem progressively blurred going down the four faces that unite them. The smallest level appears clearly to be separated from the rest, even if its edges are not clean-cut and there is a perception of relief or, alternatively, depth. In fact the upper level is in relief. Binocular vision makes it impossible to superimpose perfectly the images of the two eyes, except for the top of the ziggurat. It seems that the area of relief is brought about from a focused area, surrounded by an area that is not focused. A blurred image is an image that is indistinct, where it is difficult to define the edges. Is it the blurring that gives rise to the effect of depth? If a blurred area were painted around a square area it would simulate what happens along the sides that connect the two bases of the ziggurat seen from above and the illusion of relief should appear. These suppositions of mine are confirmed in the techniques of the artists Leonardo da Vinci and Raffaello who are commonly considered to be the forerunners of the use of shaded chiaroscuro to create the illusion of relief while Michelangelo used it to separate figures from their backgrounds violently. The artists were only imitating what focus and binocular vision do through the artifice of chiaroscuro around an area, producing the same cerebral state produced by focus and binocular vision so the same effect of relief appears. I would further point out that in all these cases, an uncertain and unsteady gradient is formed between the blurred area and the area seen clearly. Between them it is not possible to talk of edges. Is this uncertain gradient the final cause of the perception of relief? To verify this intuition take a sheet of paper with the reproduction of a leopard's coat on it and cut from one end of it the outline of a small leopard. Place this leopard on the paper: obviously it will become invisible. If I move the leopard on the paper (or vice versa), the leopard will immediately appear but in relief! This is because the background moves and becomes confused but above all the marks on the paper disappear below the silhouette of the animal and accentuate its edges in a way that is unstable. In this way it is possible to understand the illusion of relief in Kanizsa's triangle. The lp make the gradient detectors very sensitive in the normal direction to them. These pick up the disturbances and form unstable gradients, like those around the edges of the cut-out leopard; like those between the clear area and the adjacent blurred area. It is not a question of luminosity. One could think that, in the area outside the triangle, the figure is on average darker and has a gradient because of the three circular black areas. It is true and we will discuss this later but it is not the reason why there is a relief effect, which is present also in fig. 16 where the objection does not hold.

Fig. 16

The confutation that it is the unstable gradients that give the illusion of depth is supplied by fig. 17 where I have drawn in the lines around the triangle of fig. 14 and I have caused the relief effect to disappear. In conclusion, in nature a figure in relief like the ziggurat appears to be surrounded by a line of unstable gradient detectors. Inversely if I construct artificially a line of unstable gradient detectors, the figure within these gradients will appear in relief.

54

Fig. 17

4. The formation of the visual image

Tizio and I are observing the same tree from the same position. I can see the tree and I can reasonably suppose that also Tizio can see it in the same way as me. What I see in him is the tree, upside down, on his retina; but in his brain, if I could open it, I would not see any tree but lots of cells variously stimulated and variously distributed. In simple terms, if there were no stimulation of the brain cells Tizio would not see the tree, therefore those stimulations must be able to interpret how the vision of the tree is projected onto the retina. What I say now has nothing to do with the idea that it is not possible to know the world: I see the image on the retina of a man and I see the cells stimulated in his brain. Using a mechanistic method that I believe is suitable for understanding the brain, I must explain what happens in the brain and what gives rise to sight, provided that these words make sense: In the last lines of the paragraph I will discuss this claim. I believe that the seat of vision in humans is the visual cortex because a man deprived of this is blind. However a "blind vision" also exists. If a light is lit in front of a man deprived of the visual cortex, he will understand and is able to indicate with the hand the position of the light even if he claims that he cannot see it. This does not surprise me, it confirms what I have always thought: once recognition came through the chemiosensorial apparatus, vision was used to locate objects, avoid them, run after them,... this involves control of the muscles that were pertinent to the archaic visual apparatus, the one without visual cortex and, in fact, nerves are found in the thalamus that can be traced back to the eye (also to touch and hearing) and motor nerves but no nerves that go to the sense of smell. Now most of the control over the muscles has passed from the paleoencephalon (ancestral brain) to the neocortex but traces of the antique functions still remain, also in humans. However, cutting short, in humans the route of primary vision goes from the retina to the lateral geniculate body and then to the visual cortex. In the visual cortex, the associative areas, that is those connected with other parts of the brain, to nerves that control the muscles, start after the complex cells. Between the eye and the complex cells the visual system does not make any confrontations, it proceeds with the elaboration of data with its immutable procedure as do the kidneys and the liver. The comparison between the changeable data of the world and the changeable needs of the living happens in the associative area. Here it is necessary to recognise things, locate them in order to put into practice strategies to avoid them, run after them,... What information is there at this level, that is just after the complex cells? Eliminating non essential details it is necessary to remember that:

1. The complex cells are sensitive to the angles of the segments of the edges of figures and their approximate position. Referring to fig. 18 a), the segment is AB, the direction RS is that along which the segment can move within the dashed area. In other words, every segment parallel to AB within this area stimulates the same cell;

2. The contour line(or of privileged direction) spreading towards the nearby visual cells, secures the order and contiguity of the succession of angled segments;

Imagining to have a set of segments of the same length, we know the inclination (point 1 of the preceding list) and their succession (point 2). I could draw them at random on a sheet of paper as in fig. 18 b) with their inclinations, pointing out in a note that they are contiguous: I could even avoid a drawing by writing a numerical table. They are tautologies. Or I could draw them as in fig. 18 c) in order, one following the other and they would always be contiguous. In both presentations the segments are ordered, in the presentation fig. 18 b) the contiguity is specified by the note fig. 18 c) of geometric succession; the angles are the same. Images are formed in this way: marks that are uniformly grey, with a distinct edge. Vision can be interpreted as the content of information that reaches the associative area. The points listed above are certainly not the prerequisites of an axiomatic theory, everything can and must be clarified but we can't fail to see the obvious: vision is the compendium of this information, which does not produce the precise position of the segment, which, therefore, cannot be seen. Furthermore, as we will see in Cap. IV, the areas that are seen are those that receive the most stimulation and it doesn't matter how they are scattered around the brain This agrees with neurophysiology, which reveals that the destruction of this area produces blindness and with psychology according to which vision takes place in the cerebral zone where the world and the needs of the living confront each other. Optical illusions also confirm this. Combining the preceding statements with what is said about fig. 13 we understand Poggendorff's illusion in fig. 19, in which the acute angles are seen to be greater than what they really are. Now we understand not only why the two half lines, in reality aligned, appear to be two parallel half lines and because no serration appears on them. The segments on the sides must produce not only the information of succession but also that of contiguity.

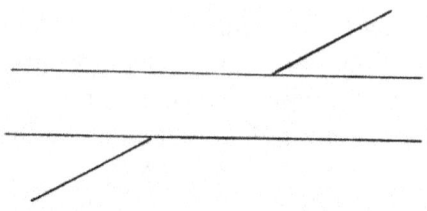

Fig. 19

The same considerations explain Hering's illusion fig. 20 a) and Zoellner's Fig. 20 b)

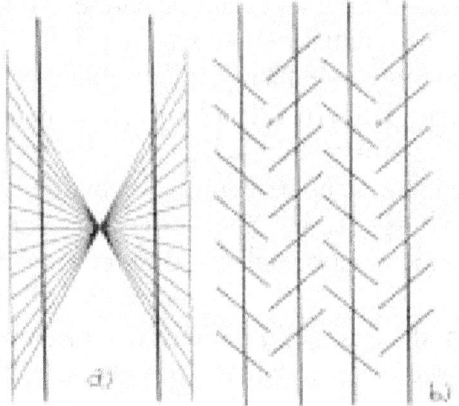

Fig. 20

In particular Zoellner's illusion makes us understand that the visual system transmits approximately the position of the edges but they are transmitted. In fact, if the vertical lines of the figure are extended beyond a certain limit they produce distortions and unstableness of the image because these vertical lines should distance themselves by virtue of the angles but it is not possible beyond certain limits. The same considerations explain unstable edges like those in Kanizsa's triangle, which appear aligned and not unstable as they are in reality, following the considerations made for fig 13 f): the complex cells do not reveal within certain limits, the position (transversal) that stimulates them. The edge of a figure is very different from a drawn line on a sheet of paper, in fact, this is seen as a thin bar and its perimeter is its edge. The edge separates two levels of stimulation. In general, within the edges luminosity is seen as constant, otherwise variations of luminosity would produce edges. Therefore vision takes place through marks of constant luminosity. A very subdued shade does not generate edges, there is no detectable gradient, a shading with a good gradient generates an unstable edge because there is no precise privileged line, the gradients overwhelm each other, they alternate in a strip and give a relief effect. This is shown in the illusion in fig. 21: the two "trapezes" have well defined external edges and also the edge on the side AB, which they have in common, is well defined. Considering the upper trapeze, this has inside, along its sides, strips of a darker shade. The most evident is along the major base line AB. If it is carefully observed we note that it is not linear. The strip forms an under-strip that is much darker next to AB and which quickly becomes lighter as it goes further from this line. The maximum gradients form a privileged line. It forms along this very dark strip within the dark strip parallel with AB. It is not a very clear strip, it is quite unstable. However, it separates the dark grey from the light grey of the strip. It is the same for the other sides of the trapeze. Therefore inside the upper trapeze, with well defined edges, a second forms with unstable edges and it also contains the shaded light grey of the strips, This is weak and does not generate gradients or its gradients are overwhelmed by the privileged line. Where the gradient is not perceived, the difference in luminosity is not perceived either, therefore it is reasonable to think that uniform brightness is formed. I would like to point out that the perception of the intensity of the shading depends on the convergence of the sensors on the retina. If the optical nerves involved in the visual process were few and distant, they would pick up gradients that thick and near tufts of nerves would not pick up. This claim will become clear on reading Chapter IV on peripheral and central vision. What is seen is approximately the average luminosity M within the confines of the gradient P-M, sometimes slightly distorted.

The same considerations apply, mutatis mutandis for the lower trapeze.

In conclusion, for what has been said in the previous paragraph, the internal trapezes lower and upper should appear in relief. The absence of ulterior gradients indicates that the visual system does not pick up shaded areas and in them the grey should be uniform. However, in the upper internal trapeze the grey is darker than in the lower and therefore should appear darker. Whoever looks at the figure can draw his own conclusions. The strip around the side AB is the main cause of the illusion. If it is covered with a finger, the luminosity of the two trapezes appears to be very similar. Greater precision in the counter-proof is obtained with a mask that covers also the shaded strips along the sides. The relief effect disappears. Another negative perception of luminosity comes from the presence of zones of different luminosity, this causes the eye to adapt to the average luminosity within the edges of the figure isolated in the central vision. A light-coloured figure will bring about a reduction in the sensitivity of the optical receptors, perhaps also a constriction of the pupil, which will darken all the area. This is provoked by the illusion in fig. 22 in which the central grey square on the right appears to be darker than the one on the left when really they are the same grey; in fact the eye adapts to the different luminosity of the two larger squares that contain them. In other words the same intensity of discharge should come from the square ABCD as that which comes from the square BAEF.

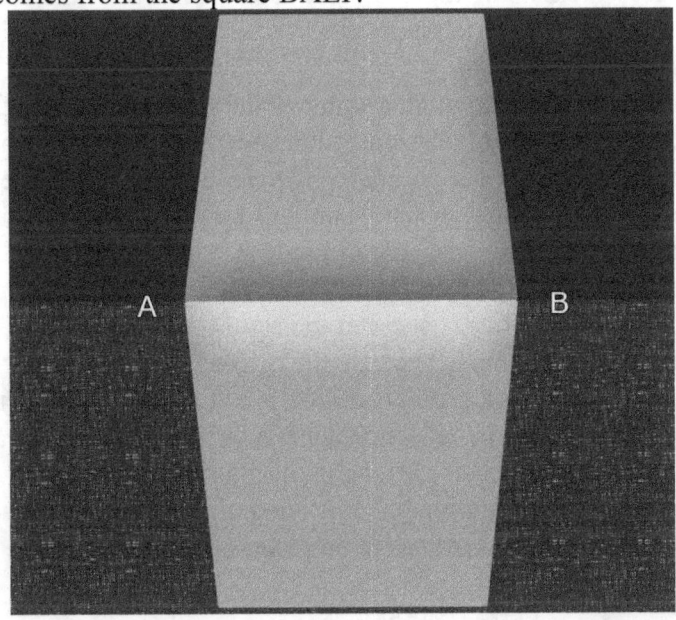

Fig. 21

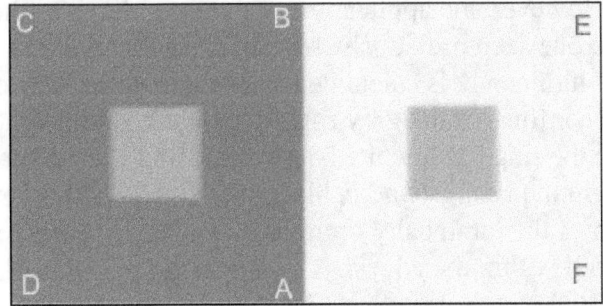

Fig. 22

This implies that the sensitivity of the receptors under the square ABCD is increased and it becomes lighter; the black is lightened but also the grey area inside it. Vice versa the sensitivity of the receptors under the white square decreases, the white becomes darker and also the grey inside it.

An interesting example which combines the regulation of brightness within edges with the adaptation of luminosity is in fig. 23 where the ring is of the same grey and remains the same grey while observing only the left side, which, instead, should likewise become lighter, observing the only the right side of the ring it should become darker. However, if I put a pencil along the direction of the separation between black and white, I see that the right part becomes darker and the left part lighter. This is because the difference of shade within the ring generates a modest gradient which is not enough to be detected and, in absence of the pencil, the visual system makes an average of the brightness of the edges, that is, in all the ring. With small corrections, already previously mentioned, there are good reasons to think that the vision of luminosity is given by the functions

$$Q=M+k(P-M) \qquad\qquad (2)$$

in particular from M because the second monomial refers above all to the edges. However, the application of the formula gives the opposite result to the one seen previously. In fact, since the circle M in which the average luminosity is calculated refering to point P, extends beyond the confines of the grey ring, it should become lighter on the right where the ring has a white background and become darker on the left where the background is black (see fig, 24). This is the information of the luminosity brought by P, then an average is made and contained within the edges.

Fig. 23

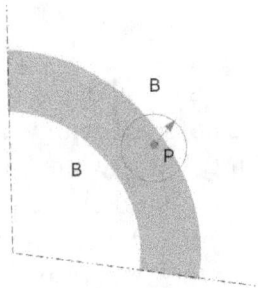

Fig. 24. B: white area

The sensitivity of the receptors, their adaptation to local luminance, which happens with the normalized intensity of discharge, is in contrast with the scope of (2). It has to do with two effects that are opposed and overlapping. The first, the one of adaptation, can be eliminated with the artifice in fig.25, in which the two sides, right and left, of the ring are in a square that has, more or less, the same average luminosity. In this case, putting the pencil as before we see that the right part becomes lighter, as expected, because it is affected by the surrounding white.

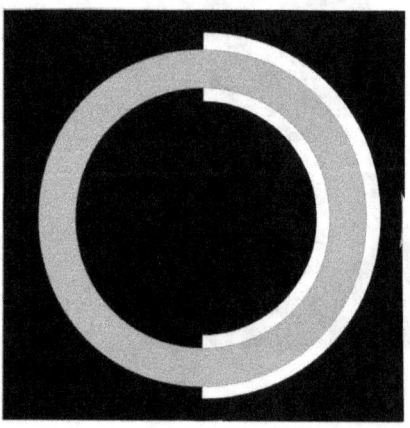

Fig. 25

Fig, 26 is further proof. The grey above and below has the same tonality but the one above bordered with white seems lighter because the M function, in proximity to the white borders but with its centre P in the grey, has high values, caused by the white which is in the circle in which the average is calculated. Instead the grey below is surrounded by black and in the points next to the edges the circle of average will be mostly black and will have a lower value, which will cause the grey to seem darker. It goes without saying that I believe that the colours in the rectangles are uniform. The change of tonality of the upper black rectangles and the lower ones can be explained in the same way. With the function (2) we can interpret the illusion in fig. 27. In fig. 27 a white rectangle appears within a series of black parallel segments which can be thought to form a square ABCD.

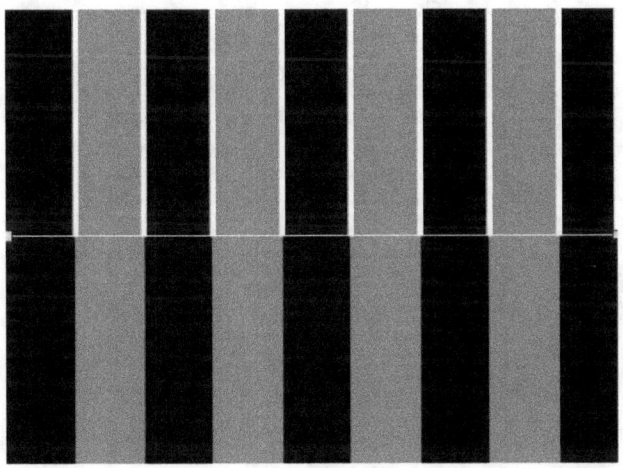

Fig. 26

We notice that between the segments of the square the brightness is less than the paper that surrounds it and the rectangle inside it, while from a point of view of physics, the white always has the same luminance. If we consider a circle of convergence with a diameter greater than the distance between the segments, the M function of every point between the lines is less than the luminosity of P, because in the circle of convergence there is the black of the lines. Moving transversely to the lines, we reach the internal rectangle and the M function diminishes until it reaches the value of P. In this zone a weak gradient perpendicular to the lines is created. The same consideration can be made where the lines end, for example on the line AB. Such gradients generate a weak, unstable edge sufficient to cause a light shading between the segments and accentuate the relief of the internal rectangle. If the reader moves further away from the page, he will see the square become darker and the internal rectangle will accentuate its relief.

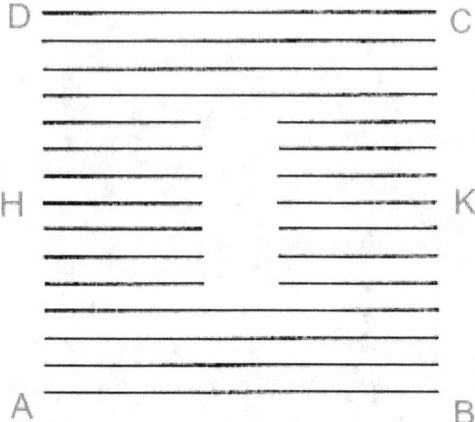

Fig 27

Based on these considerations experiments of psychophysics could be conducted aimed at quantifying (2) and the considerations on dp.

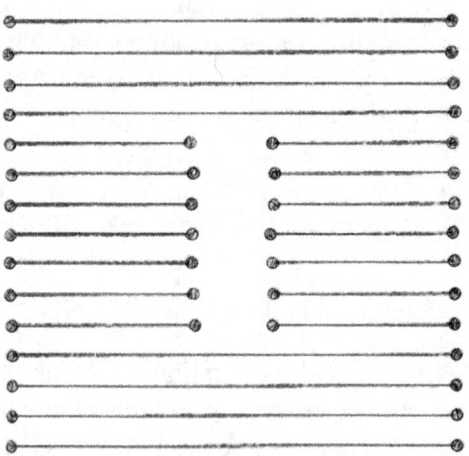

Fig. 28

If dots are drawn on the ends of the segments, as in fig. 28, the illusion disappears and only reappears on moving a good distance away because they disturb the formation of d.p. perpendicular to the lines and the light grey and white, without gradients, expands mixing together. A computer whose programmes function as I have described, you see? An image of the world forms in it as it does in me? Who knows. I don't even know if an image of the world forms in another person as it does in me. Reacts to stimulants as I do? Falls into the same optical illusions as me? This can be verified. More than this cannot be said neither of a person nor of a computer.

5. Some references to the theories of colour and neurophysiological connections

The information on colour starts off from the cones, they have vast sensitivity but maximum on the three light wavelengths. This permits us to assert that there are three types of cones whose sensitivity to the wavelengths is largely overlapping. Furthermore, each one of us, since we were children, has found out while drawing that every colour can be obtained from three fundamental colours and the theory of Young is based on trichromatic colour vision. Another theory of the perception of colours is that of Hering based on the different intensity of white and two pairs of fundamental colours, red-green and yellow-blue. Also this theory has undoubted physiological supports: the antagonist cells of the geniculate body, which receive impulses from different cones and from the system red-green and yellow-blue. In the antagonist cells the presence of red light inhibits the revelation of green light and vice versa. It is the same for yellow-blue cells. Furthermore these cells are sensitive to a range of frequencies much narrower than those the cones. In various zones of the visual system there are also non antagonist cells sensitive to colours, they seem to be the residue of a more antique vision of which I know little but the information which they take to the vision should be taken into consideration.

I agree with those who think that the two theories of Young and Hering can be reconciled: in my opinion the first is correct when limited only to cones, the second when going into the interior of the brain. Therefore if we want to explain sight, which I believe takes place in the internal part of the brain, I must give credit to the second theory. Experimenting with a video camera and computer, I noted (certainly not discovered!) that colours are an excellent system for detecting edges. In fact, if we consider two zones, one green, one red with the same luminance, the result is confused with monochromatic vision. A red filter in front of the video camera b/n makes the red zone appear white and the green zone black. In other words it generates a strong gradient of luminosity between them. The fact that edges are extremely important for recognising forms is a further indication that Hering's theory is valid. Hering, when he formulated his theory, started from the consideration that of the four colours red, yellow, blue and green, nobody had ever seen a yellow that tended towards blue or a red that tended towards green, while taking another pair of these colours and measuring the doses, it is possible to create all the hues of colours, as shown in fig. 29, taken from Wikipedia. This can be seen in colour on the site www.beva.it as well as Wikipedia. So much for neurophysiology and psychology. Also physics has something to say about light. The Sun's radiation is roughly that of a black body, around 6000 °K. In fig. 30 on the abscissae there are wavelengths (λ) and on the ordinates the intensity of that wavelength. The spectrum of the wavelengths which form visible light is only a small part of total radiation. Within the spectrum 7 colours from red to violet are usually distinguished. Following the eccentric idea of Newton who associated a musical note to every colour, he imagined that by playing and projecting the colour relative to the note, a display of light would emerge, equal in beauty to that of the music. In reality the colours fade into one another and their number is arbitrary.

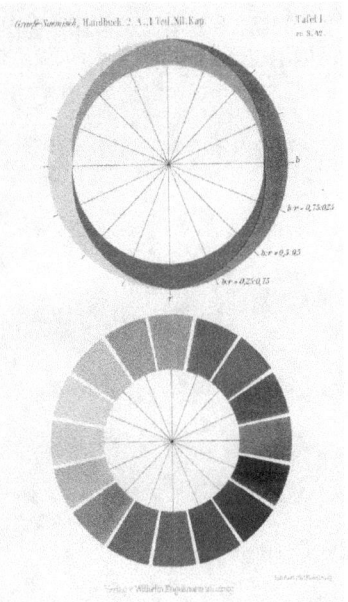

Fig. 29

Furthermore colour is a cerebral fact, a perception associated badly with the wavelength of light. Knowing this, projecting the spectrum of the Sun's light on a screen and asking observers to indicate the three fundamental colours on which Young based his theory, they roughly agree that the wavelengths expressed in nanometres are 680 for red, 580 for yellow, 550 for green and 480 for blue. Much depends on the observer, it is not precise data. To simplify the explanation, barring contrary opinions, when I speak of red I mean that particular wavelength. The same for the other colours. Before it reaches us solar radiation must cross space and enter the atmosphere where it will be partially reflected, partially refracted and partially absorbed. Without going into details which go beyond my knowledge, it is important to know that light is not absorbed uniformly compared to frequency and that the intensity of the wavelengths which strike us vary during the course of the day: just think of the light at midday and at sunset.

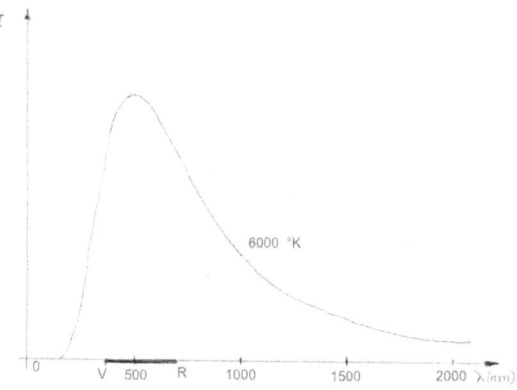

Fig. 30. VR: wavelength of visible light

Perhaps this happens because in the evening the light is more at an angle than at midday and must cross more air. Again the sky can be cloudy, etc... the light that reaches us varies a lot but despite this a white shirt appears white at midday when it reflects light whose frequencies are distributed around yellow and it appears white in the evening when it reflects light whose frequencies are principally around red. The problem of chromatic constance can be resolved, always remaining within the limits of the variations of sunlight; in fact chromatic constance is not absolute, if a white shirt is illuminated with a red monochromatic light, the shirt will appear red. At the start of these studies it is appropriate to remember that the visual system first regulates and normalises the discharge in accordance with the luminance of what is projected on all the retina (peripheral vision), in essence, on all the bright flow of light that enters the eye and then if it passes on to central vision, in accordance with the luminance of what is projected within the retinal area which is more restricted relative to central vision. We can suppose that the system for regulating colours is similar (but not identical) to that which regulates luminosity and it is necessary, also in this case, to distinguish between peripheral and central vision. In fact the cones, even if more rarely than around the fovea, are present on all the retina and can absolve the function that I will ask of them. Obviously in the adjustments necessary for chromatic vision, the pupil plays no role. Black and white vision generated by the rods takes into consideration the differences of luminosity, that is, if at that point there is more or less light. For this one channel is enough, one nerve for each point of the retina, if you prefer, that takes the information on luminosity through a discharge of more or less high frequency. Instead the nerves that reach the double opponent cells are two: one for yellow and one for blue or one for red and one for green. The intensity of the discharge of the nerve that carries the information of red from a point can be a lot or a little but it doesn't influence the discharge that carries information about green because this travels on the other nerve. While light and dark are intensities of the same light, green and red both have independent intensities. Each one of these two colours has its channel, in which the discharge is modulated with a frequency that depends on the intensity of the luminance of that single colour. It is the same for yellow and blue. The channels for the colours could be two, one for red, green and one for yellow, blue and there could be additional rules which would make this structure equivalent to that with four channels. It seems to me more complicated therefore I will think about the four channels, a hypothesis which seems to conform with neurophysiology. Also the normalisation of the intensity of frequency of discharge takes place through spatial integration and it could be thought to start from the cones. However, I believe that it would be more simple to normalise such intensity for each one of the four fundamental colours which already derive from the elaboration of the emissions from the cones. Conceptually it is possible and easy, it is enough to act on the intensity of discharge which comes from all the retina for each one of these four colours and similarly for what happens for monochromatic vision, keeping constant for each colour. In other words, for example, if peripheral vision is considered, the number of impulses per second of all the nerves that carry information about the colour blue from the visual area, must be the same, looking at a landscape both with bright sun and with clouds or looking at a green wood or the blue sea. What I have said about peripheral vision can be transposed to central vision. This hypothesis must be taken with a pinch of salt, within the limits of a biological apparatus like the brain. If, for example, one looks at a yellow scene with a very small blue area, the device will work on it but even if their frequency of discharge is greatly increased, it will not succeed with reasonable hypothesis, to reach the value needed by the normalisation. The above considerations make the visual system able to detect the gradient between the pair of colours red and green and the pair yellow and blue, also if the luminance of the coloured areas that form the pairs of antagonistic colours are the same, revealing in this way edges that would escape the notice of monochromatic vision, which generates gradients according to luminance. However the function P-M, fundamental for indicating the presence of edges in the monochromatic case, according to the intensity of luminance, is not immediately applicable in the bi-chromatic case. A gradient detector of the type in fig. 10 continues, instead, to have application. Let's think that instead of light and dark it detects red in a semicircle and green in the other. Such a detector would not pick up any gradient between the red and the blue because the nerves that take the information of the red and blue do not go to the double opponent cells. Exploring all the figure with these detectors can be tiring, but it is possible to establish a function similar to P-M and search for edges only where they are different from zero. Such a function can be obtained by making the difference P'(x,y) between the intensity of the discharge of red R(x,y) and that of green V(x,y) in every point of the visual area. M' will be the average of P' in a circle of radius r. The point P' can have a positive value, if red predominates or negative if green predominates. The (2) in this case becomes (2'). The same reasoning must be done for the pair of colours yellow and blue.

$$Q'=M'+K(P'-M') \qquad (2')$$

Similarly to what has been said for monochromatic vision. I believe that the expansion of the colours red or green is the information that M' carries and that is constant within the edges, which limit it. Otherwise a new edge would emerge. As in the monochromatic case there cannot be shading between the edges because if the leap in luminosity were perceptible, a gradient and an edge would form. Identically for the colours yellow or blue. As M' carries the visual information, in the case of polychrome it is not possible to see an area that is greenish red but bright red, dark red, black, dark green and light green. As the value of M' can be positive, null or negative and different values that are near generate the gradient. It is the same for the pair yellow blue. M' has two functions, one is red green and the other is yellow blue. In relation to the colour which they take on, if they persist in the same zone, they can generate combinations of colours. The colour yellow and green, yellow and red, blue and green, blue and red. These colours are not alternatives. Think of the information that produces the cerebral image as three overlapping transparent levels: one for luminosity, one for red or green and one for blue or yellow. In each one marks are formed, usually uniform and therefore separate from light-dark, red-green or yellow-blue edges. In our vision the information is sensed like the formation of colours in fig. 29. United with the information on luminosity the model I propose perfectly mirrors Hering's theory. The proof of this model should come from optical illusions. In fact the white shirt under any kind of light, different from that of the black body at 6000°C, will continue to appear white because if it is true that it reflects for every frequency a value proportional to the light of the environment, each one of the four colours will keep constant the intensity of the frequency of the total discharge. The value of this intensity can be arbitrary, equal or different for each colour or perhaps proportional to the intensity that the four colours have in the radiation of the black body. It is not important, it is enough that there is normalisation: This constance of the colours is amazing in the experiment that Land conducted on a picture similar to the paintings of Mondrian. Many of Mondrian's paintings are composed of squares (or other geometric shapes) in various colours, side by side. A little like the patches on Harlequin's costume (fig. 31). Land operated in this way: he illuminated a picture like Mondrian's with three projectors, one red, one yellow and one blue and viewed two rectangles, one orange and one violet. He measured the red light, the yellow light and the blue light reflected by the orange rectangle. Then he concentrated on the violet rectangle and varied the luminous intensity of the three projectors in order that the light reflected by the violet rectangle for each of the three colours, red, yellow and blue had the same intensity as that which was reflected on the orange rectangle. It was to be expected that the violet rectangle would appear orange, after all it reflected the same light that the first orange rectangle had reflected. Instead the rectangle remained violet! If we were to admit that the visual system had reformulated the sensitivity to the intensity of the light frequency, the conclusion could not appear more paradoxical. I am not sure of what I am writing because

74

the literature (that I have been able to get) which reports on the experiment is not precise. However it seems to me that he illuminated the violet rectangle of the Mondrian from in front with three lights that were altered compared to sunlight, therefore I think that the visual system regulated the sensitivity of the frequencies on the spectrum of the black body. I suggest (and if I had more time I would try it) to illuminate the Mondrian in front with sunlight, I would make the violet rectangle out of transparent paper and I would illuminate it from behind with the three projectors, in order that the same light that reflected the orange rectangle shines through it. In a context of sunlight I am convinced that the violet rectangle would appear orange.

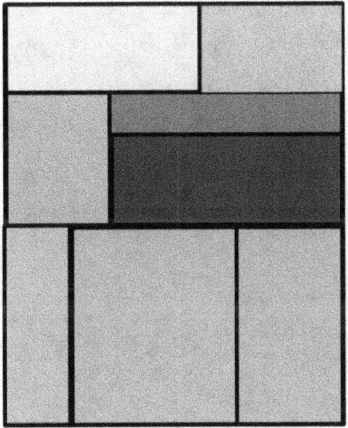

Fig. 31

I haven't made the test. I don't know if the four colours and the tonality of the grey make it possible to obtain all the hues: I would say yes, however it is for artists and photographers to speak of this. More or less the theory is correct and finds links in neurophysiology:

in the human geniculate body and in primates there are many antagonistic cells that respond to a very narrow band of few frequencies. Then there are (fewer) non antagonistic cells that respond to variations of luminance. Therefore the channels are two: one for colour and one for luminosity. I have already spoken about luminosity. About colour, only four are used, substantially four wavelengths of the spectrum and their sensitivity largely overlaps? I don't know the answers to this, I think that not even the neurophysiologists do. Probably the visual system integrates the information from all the visible spectrum and draws from it the four fundamental colours. Probably it is during this integration that the adjustments that I have described take place. I offer a workable conceptual model that ensures chromatic constance in the same way that it is ensured in the human visual system. I can't say more than that. In analogy to what is written for luminosity the fig. 32 is explained according to what is applied to colours: between the yellow lines the grey becomes yellowish and between the blue lines the grey tends to blue.

Fig. 32

A further confirmation comes from fig. 33 in which the red and green become lighter when they are crossed by yellow lines, as foreseen by Hering, in accordance with fig. 28. However, I don't exclude that

76

when opposing colours like red and green are near each other, this causes the red and green to become darker in the lower part of fig. 32. Impressive proof of the validity of the model for explaining vision comes from the experiment in fig. 34 which shows that without gradients that act as "barriers", that is they contain the information within their limits, the colours spread out.

Fig. 33

A place in the visual system where the gradients cannot form is the correspondent of the blind spot of the eye. The d.p. are vertical and we can think that they extend but there is no horizontal d.p. between the red and the green. If the square in fig. 34 is observed with only one eye so that the blind spot goes on the disc between the colours red and green you realize that the antagonist colours mix together and nobody can understand where one begins and the other ends. I have taken this illusion from the article Ramachandran which appeared in number 287 of "Science" of 1992 about which was written " The volunteers referred that when the disc fell on the blind spot, the segment appeared to be continuous, even if, paradoxically, they couldn't really see the limit between red and green." To put this into practice it is enough to cover the right eye and observe the image with the left eye at a distance of about 30 cm from the page.

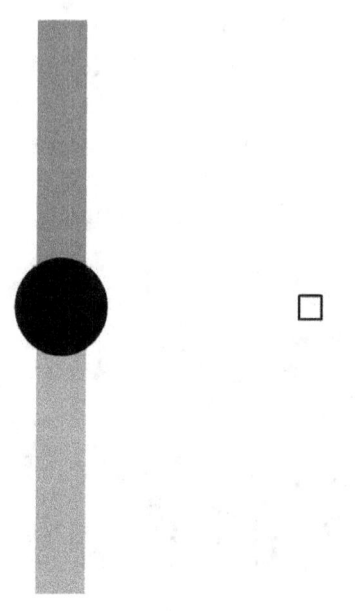

Fig 34

Fix the gaze on the small square. It is important to stare at the small square without moving the eye. Moving the head backwards and forwards, you should notice that the black circle on the left disappears and reappears alternately. This is because, when it passes through the blind spot of the left eye, the brain uses the surrounding area (completely white) to fill in the missing piece.

Chapter IV - Peripheral vision and central vision

Preliminary remarks

On considering the problem of isolating an object from its background I noticed further characteristics in the visual system. In order to understand them I have developed a model which explains the optical illusions that the brain produces. A structure of layers comes out that tends to keep constant the information coming from the isolated object. The idea of the repeated convergence of the optic nerves in a single nerve fibre comes from neurophysiology. The model that I propose develops this idea.

1. The model of isoconvergence. An outline of peripheral vision and central vision.

The dimension of the image of an object that forms on the retina sometimes is not connected to the dimension with which that object is seen. There are many optical illusions that make things appear big or small, independently from their dimension on the retina. The same reader can experiment this: put on a table two identical glasses, one at a metre from the eyes, the other at two metres. For an elementary law of optics the image of the two glasses on the retina show one glass half the size of the other glass but the two glasses appear equal! this fact is known as constancy of the form (see fig. 35). This is true if I observe the glasses one after the other but if I stand in line with them and, for example, and I concentrate my vision on the one nearest to me, I notice that the other, now blurred, seems to be reduced by half following the laws of geometrical optics. However, in the first case, the optical illusion remains.

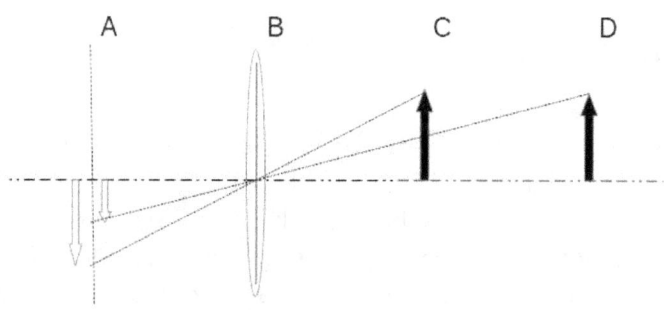

Fig. 35 A: retina, B: crystalline C,D: glasses

It is known that the receptors of the retina (cones and rods) converge differently on the fibres of the optic nerve. Without making claims to precision one can say that at the centre there is often, also only one receptor on an optic nerve. Going towards the periphery convergence increases and the sensors that converge on the same fibre of the optic nerve are always more. What is more it is known that the figures appear out of proportion in the visual cortex and that the part which falls in the centre of the retina occupies an enormous portion of the cortex while the part of the figure that falls on the periphery of the retina occupies a minimal part of the cortex. The model that I propose takes this into account. I will call it a plan model or an isoconvergence model, it will not be confused with the layered model, which elaborates the information coming from a single plane of the layered model in several layers of the layered model. Considering the nerves that come from the retina fig. 36: the circle indicated with 0 is the centre of the retina, a zone of minimum convergences of the receptors on the fibres of the optic nerve and the annuli 1,2,3,... are areas of convergence growing always greater. As the receptors, cones, rods have more or less the same area, the fibres of the optic nerve will be denser in the centre where they are subject to a lower convergence of the receptors and more rare in the periphery where convergence is at its maximum.

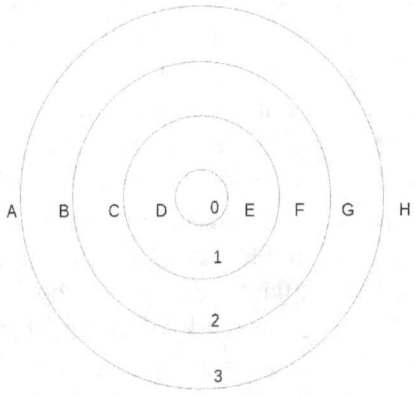

Fig. 36

The blind spot is not a part of the model and I will leave it out. In fig. 37 I propose a model of a section of the retina. The plane 0 corresponds with the circle 0 and signals start from every one of its nerves, one going towards the brain and one towards the underlying retinal planes. There are no other exits towards the the brain from this plane, only in the DE zone, which is precisely the diameter of the circle 0, in fact the plane is defined precisely by these outgoing signals. I hypothesize connections in parallel between the nerves of

81

the circle 0, which reduce the number of the nerves in a way that these have the same density of the nerves that exist in annulus 1. In the example the nerves of circle 0 of fig. 36 (DE in fig.37) are united in pairs on a single nerve. In this way these nerves will have the same density as those which come out of the annulus 1, which come from a zone of the retina in which the nerves have a greater convergence. All these nerves form plane 1 and each one of these nerves also goes to the brain, as well as the underlying plane. The pairs of nerves of plane 1 are united; the nerves obtained in this way have the same density of those that come from the annulus 2. I make these pairs of nerves start out and from those that come from the annulus 2, the connections towards the brain and I obtain plane 2. etc...etc... Without wanting to make a quantitative discourse, we can think, with reference to the previous retinal section, that every nerve of the circle 0 has its receptor, that every nerve of the annulus 1 has two receptors which converge on it, that every nerve of the annulus 3 has 4 receptors that converge on it, etc... etc... Further studies permit the convergence to be defined quantitatively. For the purposes of this text this is enough. In this context I hypothesize that the information on which the elaboration of the image is structured is taken from the nerves of a single isoconvergence plane. In fig. 37 I have marked with blue dots the attachments of the nerves which go to the cerebral areas where the image will be further elaborated. Every horizontal line of blue dots defines a plane. When a plane sends the information it contains to the brain, the function of the other planes is inhibited. I will discuss later how the visual system chooses the plane from which it receives the information, for now I take it for granted that it is possible. Having said this, I suppose that an image, for example the red arrow in fig. 38, occupies a circle of the diameter CF. It will fall in the annulus 1 and in the circle 0. The choice of plane 1 produces the vision of the complete image of the arrow. That of plane 0 would bring about a partial vision, but this part will be seen with greater detail because the density of the nerves which start from plane 0 is greater than that of the nerves that start from plane 1 and it seems natural to me to propose a proportion between the number of nerves per surface unit and detail of the image.

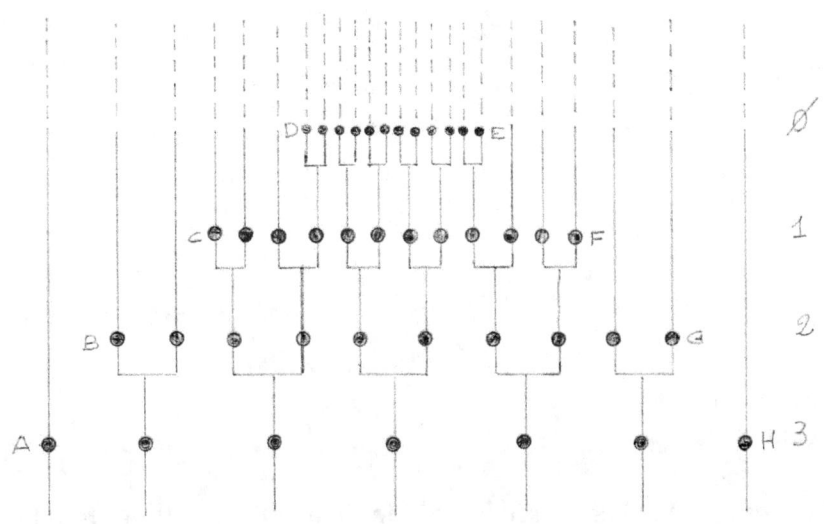

FIG. 37. Horizontal line: parallel connections: dashed line: optical nerve of the retina; 0, 1, 2, 3...: planes with reference to the annuli of fig. 36; small black circles: start of the signal towards the brain

The choice of planes 3, 4, ... would cause a vision of the arrow with little detail because it always interests fewer nerves that go to the brain per surface unit. I suppose then that it is possible to choose plane 1 (fig. 39) and inhibit the signal from all the other planes. Suppose now to move the object further away. In the case of the arrow, its image would cover a smaller area of the retina, let's say the circle with the diameter DE (see the green arrow in fig. 40). If plane 0 is chosen, the image of the arrow will have the same details as

83

before when it was nearer and covered plane 1, because the nerves that start from the two planes and go towards the brain are in the same number: confront the figs. 39 and 41.

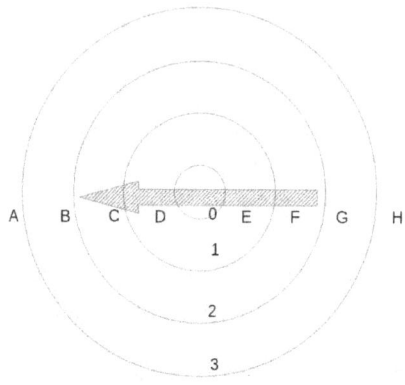

Fig. 38

If we admit that what we see is the information that, starting from the eyes, is elaborated by the visual system, it must also be admitted that the two images, that of the red arrow and that of the green arrow, even if they have different dimensions on the retina, produce the same information and therefore are perceived as being equal. This explains the illusion of the two glasses, looked at one at a time: they go to stimulate two different planes of the model and produce the same information. It also explains why, when looking at a spacious scene which covers a lot of or all the visual field, its central parts are not seen disproportionately large but exactly like the peripheral parts, despite the different convergence of the receptors on the fibres of the optic nerves.

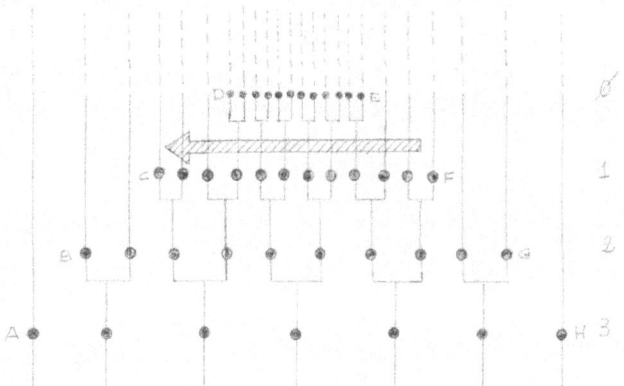

Fig 39

To realize this it is enough to observe the arrow in fig. 38, its central part is on the circle 0 but it is analyzed from plane 1 of the model which reduces the convergence of the circle 0 to the level of the annulus 1. Keeping this scheme it is possible to study various laws of convergence, different from that which I have illustrated now and how to make the convergence vary with continuity. It remains to explain in a way that is physiologically plausible and conceptually mechanizable how a plane can be chosen compared to the others. The choice of the circle on the retina determines the choice of the isoconvergence plane. For what concerns the circle, the choice derives from the gradient of luminosity or from the complementary colours that define, even if badly, the edges of the figure. above all the movement of the figure stimulates the Y cells on its border, detaching it from the background. When an image with these features falls on to any area of the retina it is conceptually possible to locate it and conceive a process for taking it automatically to the centre of the retina. I have always thought that the isolation of the object in the suitable circle of convergence was the product in most cases of movement relative to the object on its background. An animal that is well camouflaged is invisible against its background when it is motionless but appears as soon as it moves, provided that the animal and its background are not of uniform colour.

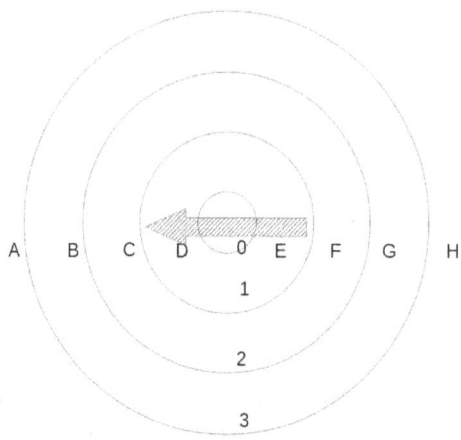

Fig. 40

Furthermore above all the movement of the figure stimulates the Y cells on its border, detaching it from the background. When an image with these characteristics falls on to any area of the retina it is conceptually possible to locate it and conceive a process for taking it automatically to the centre of the retina. I have always thought that the isolation of the object in the suitable circle of convergence was the product in most cases of movement relative to the object on its background. An animal that is well camouflaged is invisible against its background when it is motionless but appears as soon as it moves, provided that the animal and its background are not of uniform colour. The attention of small children can be attracted by moving objects in their visual field. In this case they are the Y cells that activate and I think that they are principally responsible for the isolation of an object. Or a coloured object can be put on a uniform background of a different colour, like wastepaper on a beautiful field and looking at it, the attention is immediately attracted. Here the wastepaper seems to be moving with respect to a uniform background which seems fixed and the wastepaper produces the activation of the Y cells on its edges. I have not been able to carry out experiments on this because my equipment does not pick up movement.

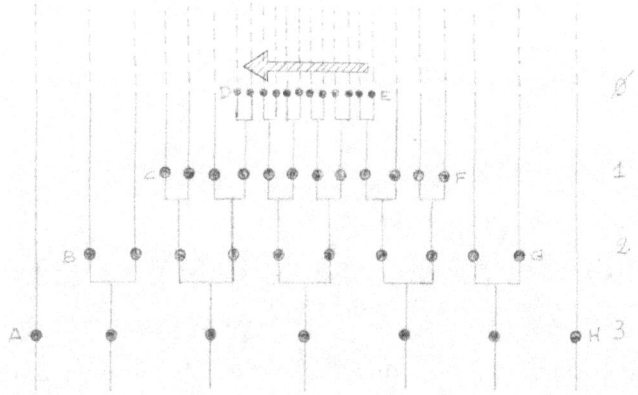

Fig 41

However, I believe that the eye is normally in a state of peripheral vision that interests all the retina and therefore the lowest plane of the model; the facts described above allow the object to be isolated in central vision. A strong gradient and movement are not the only elements that allow the object to be isolated. An object can be searched for in its surroundings, also in this case, which I will discuss later, it is conceptually possible to take the image on the retina to its centre and analyse it adequately. The choice of the plane is consequent: the image, which is understood as its stimulated edges is placed in the smallest circle that can contain all.

87

Fig. 42 shows how the arrow would appear without the hypothesis of the choice of isoconvergent planes, due to the collocation of the image in the smallest circle that can contain it: going down from plane to plane it would become smaller and smaller.

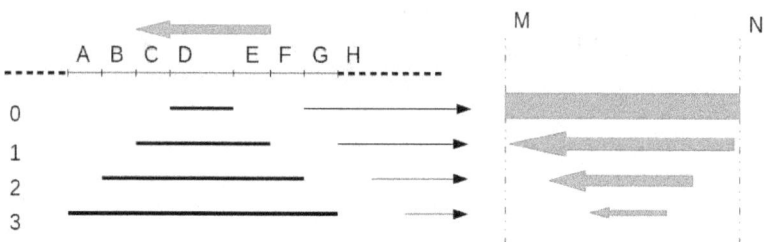

Fig. 42. A, B, C,...: retina and isoconvergence circles: 0, 1, 2, 3: planes; MN: visual field

2. Dimensions of the objects. Near objects and far objects

Observing a scene with only one eye, a near object like a glass is focused and determines a thin zone at a certain distance from the eye, more precisely the part of a spherical surface, centred on the eye in which the objects are focused and the rest, outside this distance, is blurred. It has already been said that this blurring attenuates the gradient on the edges of the figure. The narrow spherical surface that is focused can go further from the eye or nearer to it according to how the curve of the crystalline is varied by the muscle which it has around it and because with this operation its focal distance is varied. In physics this reasoning finds confirmation in the formula said to be of opticians   combined with that of the law of conjugate points. A further strategy that the visual system uses for isolating an object from its background is binocular vision: it is enough to consider the different convergence with which the

88

eyes look at a point that is near or far. Both strategies: that of focal distance and that of binocular vision also enable the measurement of the distance between the eye and the object.

This premise is necessary to surmount an apparent difficulty in the model of planes, if the visual system takes every object in the minimum circle of convergence and if this circle is matched to its plane, every object should appear with the same dimensions. How could we classify objects big, small, equal, one bigger than the other,.....?

With focus and also with binocular vision the brain knows the distance between the eye and the object and, in fact, regulates the focal distance of the crystalline. Referring to the example of the glasses, if at first I look at the near glass and then at the far glass, they occupy a different area of the retina, because the brain acts in a way that isolates the image of the glasses, taking them into the smallest circle and plane able to contain them and the glass will always seem to have the same size. However, in the brain there are two pieces of information 1) the plane has changed and 2) the distance has doubled. If a bottle was put in the place of the more distant glass, obviously bigger than the glass, the plane containing the bottle would be lower in respect of that of the glass. The bottle and glass would appear in perception as occupying all the visual field but in a cerebral comparison the bottle would be bigger than the glass, because the comparison is between planes and the distance. On the contrary if, instead, a small nut were put in the place of the more distant glass, this would also occupy all the visual field but on a plane nearer to 0. The two pieces of information: minimum circle occupied and distance from the object, allow the brain to confront the objects. Another example: if the glass that is twice as far from the eye compared to the nearer glass were double the size of the nearer glass, their image on the retina would be the same and the isoconvergence plane would be the same but the accommodation of the focal distance would allow the brain to understand which of the two glasses is the bigger. The brain has two criteria for establishing the dimensions of an object: its distance from the eye and the circle which determines the visual plane of isoconvergence contained in it.

What I say is supported by the laws of geometric optics therefore mechanizable. However, there are limits, some of pure common sense: if an enormous object is in front of the eye, it covers all the visual field and there is no regulation that holds. Inversely if an object has an image on the retina smaller than the circle of maximum convergence, either because it is far away or also because it is near but very small, it cannot be amplified further.

The proof that for comparing the dimensions of objects the brain refers to distance emerges from the following considerations. Up to now I have thought of objects that are near, let's say ten or twenty metres from the eye, instead for objects that are further away focusing is useless as their image always remains focused on the retina. Also in physics this claim can be explained with the formula of conjugated points because also varying a lot the distance of an object from the crystalline, the distance of its image from this varies very little and therefore remains focused on the retina. Binocular vision doesn't help either because in looking at a distant object the eyes remain substantially parallel. Qualitative considerations can improve the result, it remains that for distant objects in an approximate system like biological, the information of the distance is lost. So, from my house the little mountain which, despite its relatively modest dimensions, is called Gran Turou (read as in French) is 1355m high and distant three or four kilometres but it appears bigger than the majestic Monviso 3841m and a few dozen kilometres away. The law of constancy of form is not valid any more for mountains like it is valid for glasses, for our hands, because there is no longer information about the distance. Therefore as a result it is impossible to compare two distant objects "by eye", one far away, the other not so far, and understand the dimensions. It is possible to measure mountains, the Sun, the Moon but with geometry. Ancient peoples were convinced that the Sun and the Moon had the dimensions that they saw. It is necessary to explain how big a star is to a child, otherwise he will think it is the same as a firefly, whereas he does not confuse which animal is the bigger between a cow and a cat. All these arguments take into account the consideration that comparison is an event that takes part in the brain between two perceptions because a single perception brings every object to be seen with the same dimensions. The brain combines the information of the plane and the distance of the object and draws its conclusions on the dimensions. These considerations also cause some optical illusions and are in agreement with the idea of the convergence of the nerves in the visual system.

3. Comparison between figures and optical illusions

For the purpose of comparison the brain also takes into account the information about distance. Obviously if the figures are drawn on a piece of paper, and I will start considering this case, they are at the same distance from the eye, therefore this factor does not need to be considered. All the figures are brought to occupy the entire visual field by being made larger or smaller and in this case it is not a phenomenon of geometric optics. In fact the figures have different dimensions on the retina, but it is the observation of the figure through optic nerves, having a smaller or greater convergence. In order to effectuate the comparison between the figures which appear to all be equal because they are brought to occupy the entire visual field, it is necessary to invert the law of convergence and scale down what has been artfully enlarged. With regard to this, I have elaborated a hypothetical model to explain this cerebral work. A first

91

rough draft of this is in fig. 43 where, instead of using arithmetic, it seemed clearer to me to show my reasoning with geometry. Given two segments AB and CD, one the double of the other, supposing (for now, in a first draft!) that they interest two retinal circles which have a diameter, one the double of the other, each segment will appear equal, occupying all the visual field, represented by the area between the two dashed parallel lines in fig. 43 c). AB, the smaller segment, will be placed on a high plane and CD, the larger, on a very low plane. In fig. 43 c) the visual field has a width of CD, the larger diameter and therefore AB with the smaller diameter has been doubled. In the construction AB is at a double distance from O in respect to CD, this means that on any line PP' the proportions of the two real segments are conserved. In the construction the distances from O are inversely proportional to the width of the visual circle. The model in fig.43 is, however, a first draft in that the width of the visual field and the dimensions of the figure coincide. It is never like this; in fact the figure is isolated and taken in scale in a zone between the eye and the brain before a precise edge is formed, which, moreover is formed of memory retention not of perception. In that cerebral zone the edge of the figure is thick, it is the first result of lateral inhibition, more or less like in fig. 12a). I don't know in which precise zone of the brain the process is carried out because it is repeated in several zones. However, the isolation of the figure from its background precedes the formation of edges, above all it is due to movement; in fact, in the vision of babies only a few months old, the figures don't have completely formed edges but they know how to collocate figures in space. Some studies of neurophysiology claim that the anisotropy of the expansion of inhibition, that takes place starting from a point generates an elliptical figure, with the major semi-axis horizontal. I have no ideas about the eccentricity of this ellipse and I can't find the article of thirty years ago that referred to the discovery any more. However it is not very important, even if the propagation of the inhibition were circular there would be no consequences on what I will say.

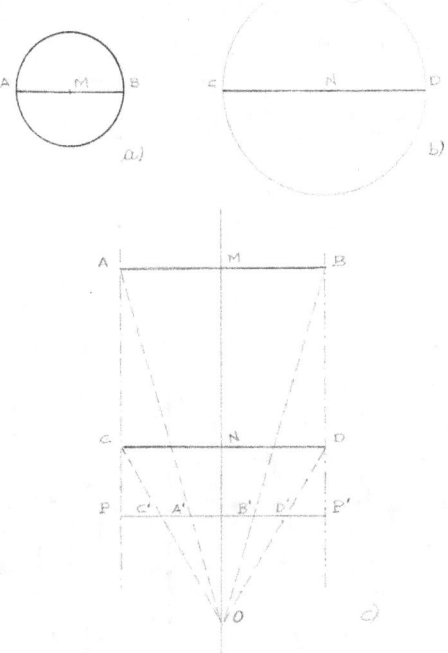

Fig. 43

Secondly the inhibition, wherever it takes place, happens beyond the retina R (ref. Fig. 44), in a zone I where the convergence of the receptors on the same fibre of the optic nerve has already taken place. An inhibited areola of I which interests the nerves which arrive from the centre of R is projected as a small area on R. Instead the same areola of inhibition of I but which interests the nerves at the periphery of R, projects as a large zone on R. This is a consequence of the different convergences of the receptors on the optic nerves.

Therefore an inhibited areola interests different retinal areas, smaller in the centre, greater in the periphery of the retina. As a consequence the figures which occupy a greater area of the retina, because they are nearer to the eye or because they are physically bigger, will have around them the projection of a greater inhibition halo than the smaller ones. In fact there is no reason to think there is a difference of thickness of the edges in I, the phenomenon is the same.

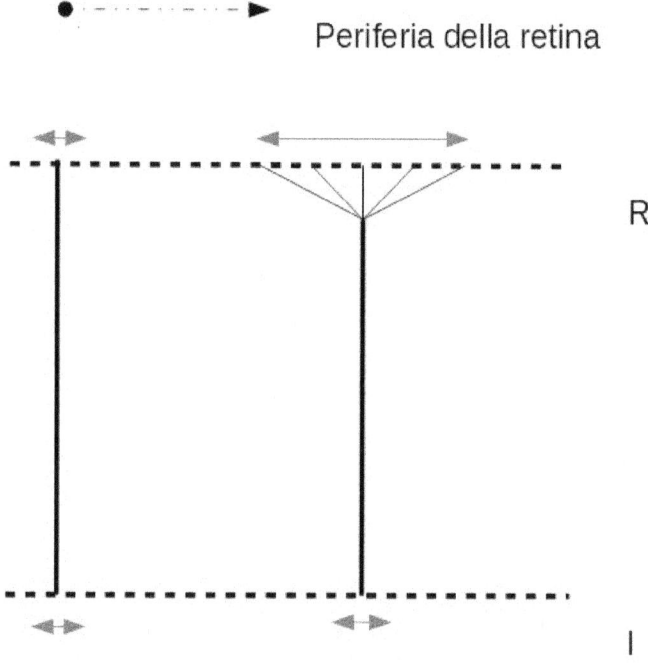

Periferia della retina

R

I

Fig. 44

These observations allow the model in fig. 43 to be improved and to discuss some optical illusions.

94

One of these is in fig. 45 in which the two shaded circles are equal but the one on the right seems smaller. The circles include vertical segments in them in figs. 45a) and b) and, as previously said, the distance BK<DK'. In the construction fig. 45 c) ON is proportional to the radius NK in fig. 45a) while OM is proportional to the radius NK' of fig. 44 b). CD occupies all the visual field defined by the parallels with dashed and dotted lines of fig. 45 c) and HG is the diameter of the internal circle: Also AB occupies all the visual field, as it has been enlarged proportionally and EF is the circle that has also been proportionally enlarged. Projecting the two circles on the segment PP' it is possible to understand how the two circles are not perceived to be equal, but the one in fig.45 a) seems bigger.

In fig. 45 I distinguish between circles of convergence and visual field, a distinction that was not there in in fig. 43. The diameters of the circles of convergence MK and NK' determine the segments OM and ON, which are inversely proportional to them. The distances AB and CD are brought to occupy all the visual plane and not the part that they occupy in the circle of convergence. In this way disproportion is generated, even if it is inherent in the equal height of the lateral segments of the two shaded circles. A summary of this is shown in fig. 45: the dashed triangle is the figure that is projected onto the retina. This is because the greater annulus falls in a retinal area more peripheral than the minor one. The two circles of convergence will have disproportionate radii, which are reflected in the distances OM and ON of fig. 49 and in the geometric model it is clear because fig. 48 a) is greater then fig. 48 b). The illusion of Mueller-Lyer in fig. 50 can be explained in the same, identical way. Also here AB appears to be smaller than CD, because the retinal circle that surrounds the bigger figure below, is disproportionally greater than the circle that surrounds the higher one.

95

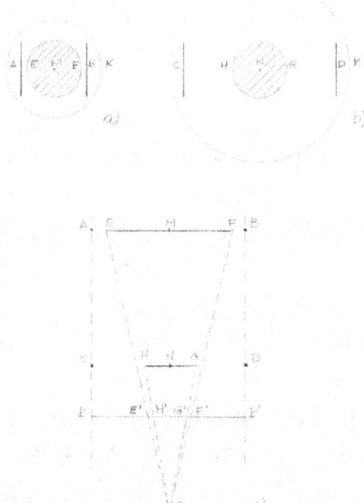

Fig. 45

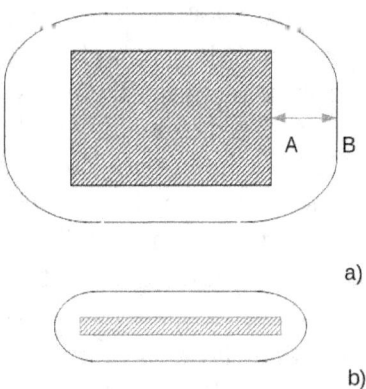

a)

b)

Fig. 46

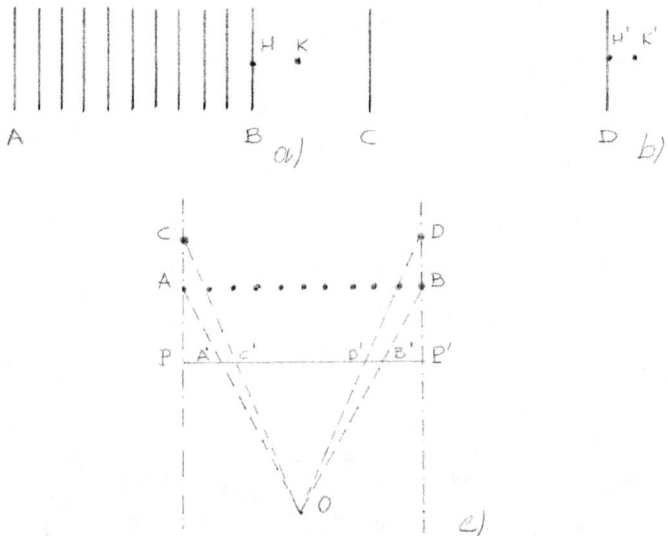

Fig. 47

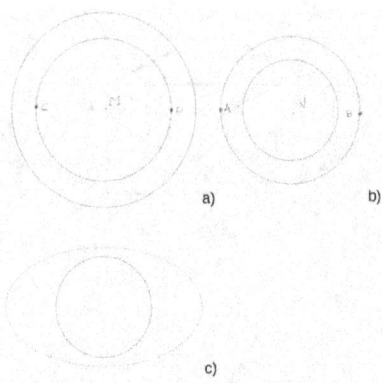

Fig. 48

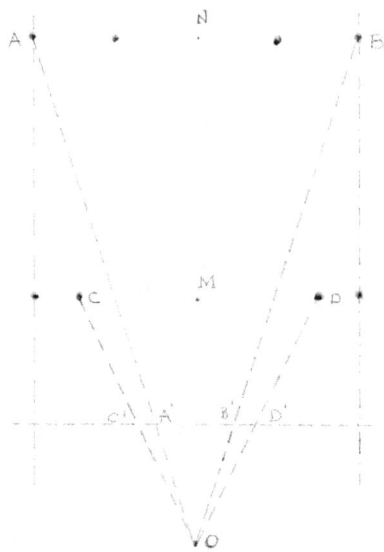

Fig. 49

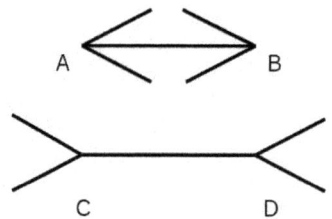

Fig. 50

Chapter V – The topological recognition of forms

Preliminary remarks

A classical method for recognizing forms is to utilise certain particularities of them like having points in certain positions, having straight edges in certain positions of their perimeters, present holes in certain zones, having a certain ratio area perimeter...., each one of these features can be seen as a dimension of a space and a specific form, defined by the value of its features, it is seen as a vector in this space. Then it is possible to say that two forms belong to the same class if the vectors that form them do not differ beyond a certain size. I was nineteen and thought this approach was weak because it resulted in a thicket of complex mathematical formulations instead of paying attention to what were the features that could describe the forms. The ones that I saw in use were "ad hoc", functional for one class of objects but not in general. I spoke to professors about this but they told me that I was posing a problem that was not essential. They were in love with mathematics and couldn't see the void underneath. In my opinion, instead, whoever wished to recognise all the forms had to understand what were the features that would make it possible to reach this goal.
I don't like thinking about details and, even though I was not rich, neither was I oppressed by economic reasons to construct and sell machines that were useful for specific industrial uses. I started from far behind, I could do it, at that time I had really a lot of time in front of me. Also time for discussing politics and religion, time for walking alongside the river Po, in the Langhe, the afternoons and

evenings seemed endless. Time for love, time for looking at the sky and the stars, the view blocked in part by the Saint Anastasia chapel, smell the perfume of the fields, listen to a dog barking in the distance. Naked, beautiful in our youth, happy with what we could give ourselves. We didn't feel these same sensations again in the same place after fifteen years. Alone and unhappy, stupidly we tried to find them again. I smile to think how little I was inhibited. You too have made these comparisons.

It didn't work.

It was the last time.

However, all this never distracted me from my studies of the brain, much less my official studies of physics, to which I devoted marginal efforts: I philosophized a lot to have a framework of reference to guide me and I didn't let myself fall into the misguided search for an immediate result. I came to the conclusion, as I have already stated, that we cannot know the world external to the brain, but the brain must be able to make predictions. How is it possible to design senses that connect the world and the brain if nothing is known of the world the senses want to explore? There is no possibility of reasoning. In fact, nature has provided through natural selection, forming senses (and the brain) suitable for this purpose and they succeed in making these predictions (with good possibility). In humans the main sense is sight and predictions start with recognising forms which, in my opinion and in agreement with Piaget, occurs first in a topological way and then it is refined in a syntactic way. Always in my opinion, the first way is typical also of superior animals: The term topological, which I use because Piaget used it, is not to be understood in the extended sense that it has taken on in mathematics, but rather in its intuitive and primogenital significance of the geometry of a sheet of rubber or geometry of the continuous. Indeed also this meaning must be limited: the brain must recognise as belonging to the same class

those figures that a child less than three years old says are similar. In the following paragraphs
I will try to mechanize this idea of similarity: For those who are not experts in the processing of images on computers I will say that the devices for studying forms are carried out connecting a video camera to a computer which, limited to the vision of black and white, transforms the image on a screen to many small adjacent and ordered squares, each one of which has a shade of grey. In parallel, we speak of a matrix (table) of pixels (small squares) each one of which has a position, defined by its coordinates and a value, a level of grey. If the same object is rotated, transferred or moved further away from the video camera, it produces different images and, in parallel, a different matrix of pixels. How can the computer recognise that the object is the same if the matrix of pixels is different? For as long as it deals with rotating, transferring or reducing (provided that it is in scale), it is not difficult to make the computer understand that it is dealing with the same object. These transformations are said to be linear and are known in mathematics, it is enough to apply them to the programmes but if two objects are slightly different, like two letters of the alphabet in a different typographic style, there is no general way, only a series of ad hoc artifices that function for the Latin alphabet but the same artifices don't function for the Arab alphabet. This is a problem that has persecuted artificial vision since the end of the 1940s. Reflecting on this argument, as I was nearing my 28 years, an idea came to my mind that even now I place at the base of my system for recognising forms. I thought about an arrow like the one in fig. 51, its rotation, its change of position and its reduction in scale would not have influenced its angles, therefore if I used these to describe the figure, I would save the heavy calculations necessary for following the linear transformations. This was no small thing, furthermore, because the idea was valid for linear transformations, why not try it out, with appropriate improvements, at the base of a

101

general recognition of forms? I looked for correspondence to these ideas of mine in literature on the subject and found that Attneave considered angles essential for recognising forms. Attneave's "cat" in fig. 52 is famous. It is unmistakably a cat and all the information comes from the angles. I then found the work of the neurophysiologists Hubel and Wiesel and knew I was going in the right direction.

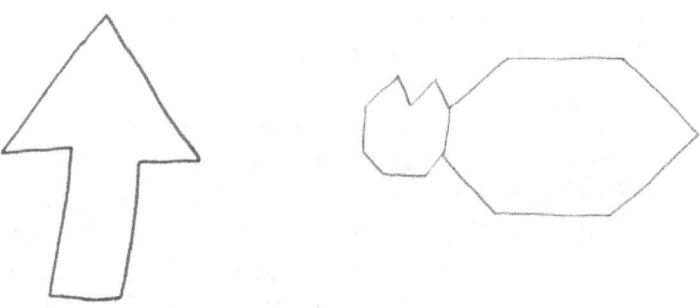

Fig. 51   Fig. 52

I noticed that the angles of an arrow drawn on a sheet of rubber pulled in unpredictable directions, change their values and if they exceed a certain limit, together with the change of the values of the angles, the drawn figure loses the form of an arrow in the sense that a child would no longer recognise it as such. The limits of the deformation of the figure so that it generates another that is similar are limits on the variation of its angles. This does not contrast with the function of the brain because Hubel and Wiesel discovered that cells that respond to bars of light of a determined inclination continued to do it until the inclination of the bars varied between 10 – 15 degrees, beyond this approximation other cells responded. Furthermore the cells that responded to a bar continued responding if the bar was moved within a certain limited area. I applied this idea to the computer. I can say that more or less after I had extracted the edge (the perimeter) of the figure, I measured its angles in the order that they were found on the perimeter and then I compared them with other, similar series, taken from previous figures. I memorized them on a table until I found, if it existed, the one that corresponded or rather the one that had angles within the aforesaid approximations equal to the one present on the computer. I immediately understood that in the two figures, that a child considers to be similar, there were different details and because of this their order of angles was different and that the computer would not succeed in recognising the equal parts and establishing that the two forms belonged to the same class. It was necessary to eliminate the details that had little importance and get to the "essential forms", that is a series of angles and positions that were identical for all the similar figures. The expression "essential forms" is not empty rhetoric, as it may seem, it will be defined operationally. For this I constructed a "layered model", layer after layer the figure lost its unimportant details and came closer to the essential form. In the first years of the 1980s I used and, allow me, invented a method of representation of a hierarchic type of information, now (in the year 2019) it is very popular and goes by the name of "deep learning". Two problems arose 1) How to make the computer distinguish the unimportant details of the form and 2) within the heirachic representation of information, always more abstract, layer by layer, how could the computer chose the "essential form". For the first problem it was natural to resort to angles. I realised that it was possible to define the power of an angle and that this was also the measure of the importance of the detail of the figure. In the layer model, little by little the less powerful angles of the figures were eliminated. The figure was schematized until it reached its "essential form" and beyond because the process continued and reached, if the starting

103

figure was closed, the form of a triangle, the most general of the closed figures, whatever initial form it had. About the second problem, the choice of the layer to be considered as containing the essential form could take place only through the teaching or the experience of the machine and, as will be seen later, it can be mechanized.

From the 1940s of the last century much has been discussed of neuronal networks, of perceptron, that were not very different from the neuronal networks, principally about the recognition of forms. In all these devices connections between "neurons" that were rewarded or depressed based on teaching were foreseen. This approach gave unsatisfactory results and for decades the argument was shelved, to be taken up again about twenty years ago, more or less in the same terms but using calculators that were much more powerful. I think that the fundamental idea of perceptron is correct but incomplete: the problem is always the same, the lack of definition of the features. To recognise forms, the features, at least the principal ones, in my opinion, are the angles and in order to define the essential form I have applied the idea of the neuronal network, rewarding the features that are equal in each class of forms.

The neuronal (or neural or neuronic) networks function well with the particular features of a class of images, with angles it should function for each image. The purpose, the hope is to achieve a "general purpose" system of recognition, as already said, that is "human like". I am not saying that angles are the only characteristic that make it possible to achieve the recognition of forms but I think it is basic. Other features such as colour, dimensions can be useful for the recognition of forms but in a subordinate position to angles. This is limited to the sense of sight because in humans smells and tastes,... that come from the other senses are also subordinate.

1. The power of angles

In cats there are cells in the visual cortex that respond to bars
inclined in various ways within the cat's sight. If the inclination of
the bar is varied for about ten degrees the cells that respond will vary.
Certainly one can say that such cells are sensitive to angles but not to
the angles to which we are accustomed in their geometrical
significance, having two sides and a vertex. However, there is a link
between angled bars and angles, in fact considering fig. 53 it is clear
to all that around the perimeter there is a highly stimulated external
strip, always next to the perimeter, but internally there is a highly
inhibited strip. This is because of the lateral inhibition phenomenon.

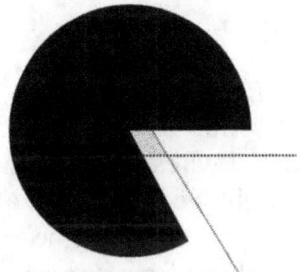

Fig. 53

Around the vertex of the recess, external to the figure, the two
stimulated strips unite giving rise to a maximum of stimulation, the
shaded polygon in the figure. Also, without going deeply into the
function that is the sum of the stimulation, it is possible to say 1) it is
greater the more the angle is acute and 2) it only exists if both sides
are sufficiently long. Think of an acute angle with a long side and a
very short side, the stimulated strip on the long side is also long but
the one on the short side is short and the sum of the stimulated strips,
which takes place near the vertex of the angle is only as long as the
short side. Therefore the stimulation on the vertex of an angle with

105

(at least) one short side is modest. The sum of the stimulations of the two strips on the sides of an obtuse angle is also modest. They diverge and add up only very near the vertex. These considerations make it possible to define and measure the power of an angle as the value of the stimulation around its vertex. Since the power of the angles is associated with the importance of the details of the figure, the criteria is obtained for establishing which are the details which are more, or less important. In fact an obtuse angle curves a straight line only slightly, an acute angle with one or two short sides generates a modest recess or projection. It is not so with an acute angle with long sides, this is a detail of the figure that receeds or protrudes a lot.

2. The layered model

In this paragraph I will describe how I actualized the ideas expressed in the preceding paragraph. I will start by noting that the toys of small children are very brightly coloured and often move in order that they can discern the edges, above all the external ones, which permit them to isolate the object from its background. These edges are, given the premises, closed, continuous and I will think of them in that way now. Not that this is indispensable, neither in the brain nor in my apparatus which simulates it. However it simplifies learning. I obtain the edges with the method previously explained and once having them, I inscribe a polygon on them with very short sides and which are very near the perimeter. Then I go on to evaluate the power of the angles of this polygon with a method that quantifies the propositions of the previous paragraph. The two cases in fig. 54 a) and in fig. 54 b) deal with angles that have little power and which are eliminated and substituted by a straight line. The angle B in fig. 54 a) which is almost flat or extremely obtuse is eliminated and substituted by the dashed segment AC. In the case of fig. 54 b) the angles B and C have little power because they have a short side: Both are eliminated and the line ABCD is substituted by the segment AD. It is clear that the line will have sides that become longer and longer and unequal. The procedure is repeated until the figure, if it is closed, becomes a triangle.

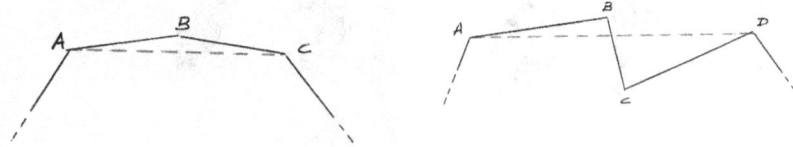

Fig. 54 a   Fig. 54 b

The value of the threshold of power of the angles of the line increases progressively and with every increase the typical values of the line are registered on a table, which constitutes a matrix. I have called "layered model" all the matrix of the table which contain information about the edges of the figure which is progressively generalized. The information contained in the layers is hierarchical. I have called "contraction" the operation with which I eliminated angles, contracted the lines that were obtained and also the numerical tables equivalent to them. Finally I called the set of contracted lines "configuration". Fig. 55 shows four different forms of the capital letter R of the Latin alphabet. The forms could be different, the result would be the same. In figure 56 the result of the procedure is shown, applied to the form bottom left of fig. 55. It follows alphabetical order from the letter a) where there is the original form to the letter o) where there is the triangle that all the closed forms are reduced to. As can be seen the form, contraction after contraction, loses more details, that is, it acquires more generality until it becomes a triamgle. The figs. 56 h), 56 i) and 56 l) are particularly interesting because they represent the essential form of "R" and are common to all the "R" that a child would say are similar.

Fig. 55

The figure 56 appears from all the similar "R" with 6 angles two concaves and three convexes and 6 sides. The value of the angles and the measure of the sides are not equal, they vary according to the shape of the initial "R" but the computer must recognise them as equal, even in these approximations. This will be the argument of the following paragraph, for the moment it comes spontaneously to me to point out that the successive contractions are characterized by lines with sides that become longer and longer and angles that are more and more accentuated. The method of contraction can be seen as the opposite of the method of "smoothing". In order to complete the picture I include the results of the processing of the other three forms in fig 55. The essential forms are indicated with a white dot.

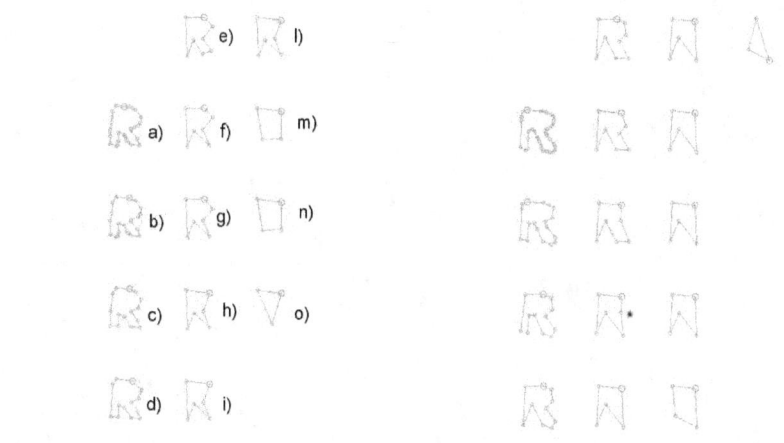

Fig. 56   Fig. 57

109

Fig. 58   Fig. 59

Also fig. 57 has its essential form, in fact it has 6 angles indicated
with a small circle. I would like to point out that an identical essential
form for all the similar forms is a goal that cannot always be reached,
like the identity of the configuration after the essential form.In the
following paragraph I will discuss how the figures can be recognised
also with configurations that are not perfectly equal.

3. Recognition and learning

In this paragraph with the words " recognition of forms" I mean the
capacity to recall two similar forms with the sense that a child of
three would give to this expression. As a child would say that
the four forms of fig. 55 are similar, the machine must learn, also
seeing only one of them, to recognise the others as similar to the first.
if the name "erre" has been given to it, the machine must be able to
remember this when the others are presented to its visual apparatus.
This result can be obtained comparing the contracted lines. For

110

recognition it is essential to remember the observations of Hubel and Wiesel, according to whom the same simple cell of the visual cortex responds to an angled bar within a certain approximation and within a certain area. According to this criteria, the contracted lines of the figs. 56, 57, 58 and 59, marked by the black dot are "equal" and in reality come from similar forms, to which could be given the same name. Since the machine captures this similarity, we are on the track of a human like recognition. I won't bore the reader with mathematical demonstrations that I carried out and which have led me to conclude that a description of forms through angles and their position, the configurations, that is, the hierarchical structure between contracted lines is extremely important for recognising the figure. It is enough to think that from two essential forms that are perfectly equal, going down through the process of contraction, further equal contracted lines and therefore equal configurations. It is not like this if the essential forms are only approximately equal like the essential forms of R. In fact the corresponding angles, despite being in approximations, are more or less powerful and are contracted one after the other. Information is taken from the successive contracted lines, especially on the proportions of the figure which escape an analysis of the sole preceding contracted line. It is obvious that mathematics is a tautology and therefore all the information is already in the essential form in the value of its angles, in the length of its sides. At the limit it is all in the form and all the process of contraction could be thought in another way. I follow models that help my intuition. Closed this parenthesis, it is necessary to learn how to compare contracted lines. In order that the comparison between two contractions resulting from different figures is made easy it is necessary that the figures are normalized. In fact for recognition not only the angles are important but also their position. The operation of normalizing was discussed in detail in Chapter IV. I have not been able to simulate the plane model because it would require hardware superior to that which I own and availability of time that I did not have. I made up for this by normalizing the length of the perimeter, then I started to inscribe a polygonal with very short sides on it which approximates it excellently. I assigned distances to its vertex, understood as the length of the polygonal from its initial point, which is always the highest point on the left of the figure. The initial point of the polygonal coincides with its final point, because normally the polygonal is closed. I assume not to make the figure invariant in rotation unless advised otherwise. Anyway it is "human like", in fact a tree has a different significance if it is standing up or has fallen down and also the significance of the letters p,d,q,b change with rotation. In short the invariance of rotation, to the inversion of contrast, to linear transformations...., are ideas that are a legacy of mathematics whose application can lead to unforeseeable disasters. In nature a cat and a tiger, even if they are only different in scale, are not the same thing. The comparison between the configurations happens between the current figure, that is the figure that is present in the visual apparatus of the computer, and the configuration of all the other figures that have been memorized, each one of which has its own name. The current figure will be recognised from the best correspondence between its configuration and a memorized one. The memorized configurations can be refined with the methods of the neuronal network, making an average of the elements of configurations derived from similar figures. However, I have noted that the result of recognition is equally precise without having to resort to refining memorized configurations. It is enough to memorize the configuration of a figure, not misaligned, a good sample of its class and the computer will recognise the similar figures. This surprised me and comforted me. The comparison between the configurations is a complicated procedure. It starts with a comparison between contracted lines, in order to understand if they are completely or partially equal, with regard to a contracted line of the current figure in fig. 60 a), and the comparison with the contracted line of the memorized figure in fig. 60 b). For greater clarity of presentation I have preferred to draw the contractions, rather than write their numerical value. As a first step I connect the angles that are approximately equal between the two contractions. Generally each angle is connected with various angles that are approximately equal to it. I choose by convention to measure the angles from the internal part of the figure which can be imagined to be the profile of a head. Observe fig. 61 in which the perimeters of the two profiles have been developed. As an example we pay attention to the three angles D, F, H, of the fig. 60 a) and we consider senselessly large approximations, for example: the angle D measures around 90°and can be connected with A', B', D', G', I', and L', which have approximately that value. The angle F measures about 270° and connects with C', F', and H'. The angle H measures more than 270° and connects with C', F',and H'. Note that H' connects both with F and H. As a second step, it must be noted that the segments AB and A'B', BC and B'C',... are not very different one from the other while the origin of the lines from which the measures proceed can be different. It is for this that in fig. 61 I have located the point A' more to the right than point A and note that the lines which connect the vertex of the corresponding segments are "more or less" parallel because the corresponding segments have more or less the same length. The corrected lines of connection are, usually, angled in the same way for all the figure and in the case of disproportions between the current form and the memorized one zonal stripes of straight lines form more or less parallel, if there is an area of the figure only moved or also convergent if the area of the figure were made smaller, etc....

Figs. 60

Leaving aside, for the moment, these particular cases, I wish to point out that the parallelism of the straight lines, which indicates that the segments of the two polygonals, current and memorized, are equal, is of great help in choosing the elements for connecting. Using as criteria the sum of the powers of the angles of the connected elements it is possible to sum up the powers of all the connected angles with a certain direction, then other connected angles with another direction and so on....., a histogram is formed from which the angulation with the maximum power emerges: it is the one I was looking for, which I will call privileged difference between the lengths and I will refer to it to evaluate the correct connections between the angles of the current form and the memorized one. In fig. 61 the connections which are accepted because they are angled correctly are in thick lines. With this simple criteria it is noticeable that also the links HF' and FH' are angled (within a certain approximation) correctly, why exclude them? The angles of the forehead, the eye, the nose,... like their distances can be widely modified and everyone will agree that it is still a profile. It is not so

114

with their order, the nose cannot go above the eye, the mouth below the chin: the angles have an order. This assumption implies that the connections chosen from fig. 61 cannot cross each other. If they cross, the connection between the most powerful angles is chosen and with the connection nearest to d.p.

In choosing to eliminate the connections the algorithm takes into account both criteria. Another criteria which is used for choosing between the connections are the bisectors of angles. The bisectors are orientated, therefore the values of their angles cover the turn (full circle). The bisector of D is equal to that of A',D',and I' but not to B' G' and L'. The connections of these last three angles are eliminated, a fortiori. For the same reason the connection HF and also FH' would be eliminated. Also for the bisectors the idea of the difference between those of the corresponding angles is valid: it must be constant, in the case of the two figs. 60 a) and b) near to zero. If a figure were rotated in respect to the other the difference between the bisectors of the corresponding angles, still constant, would not be equal anymore to zero. A histogram is formed also for the bisectors and a privileged difference is found between the bisectors that will allow the connections that deviate from it to be excluded. The two criteria, the privileged difference between the sides and the privileged difference between the bisectors, are used before the third criteria, that of the order of the angles, which in this way has a very modest use. The lengths between which the difference is made are not the lengths of the sides of the two polygonals: in that case this difference should be near 0 (without considering the case of disproportions), but between the length of the polygonal of the current figure between its starting point and an angle, let's say the angle B and the corresponding length O'B' of the polygonal of the memorized figure. Consider the length OB and compare it with the various lengths O'A', O'B', O'F',... of the memorized figure which have angles approximately equal. The sought for constant emerges

from the histogram of the differences OB-OA, OB-O'B',
etc...Graphically this is the angulation of the connections between the
developments of the two contracted lines in fig. 61. It is understood
from this which are the corresponding angles.

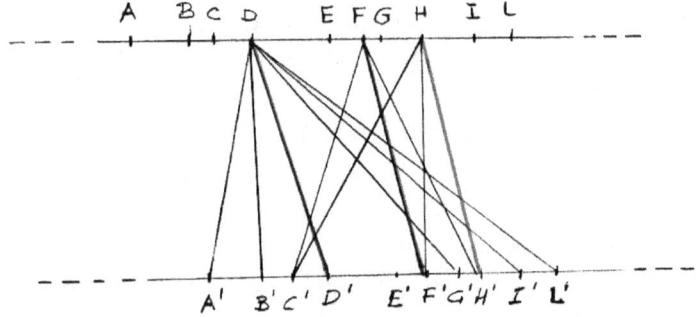

Fig. 61

The simple difference between the sides does not carry this
information like it does not carry the difference of the bisectors. For
the bisectors the difference of their values, which must be constant, is
sought. This information can be used to perfect the choice of the
corresponding sides which is done with the difference of the lengths.
The two configurations, current and memorized are formed of many
layers, each of which contains a contracted line, How can the
contracted lines of the layers be compared? The third with the third,
the fifth with the fifth, the umpteenth with the umpteenth. Comparing
layers with some depth is not a senseless idea, because as the figures
have been normalized and the coefficient of contraction is constant in
every layer, there is the same loss of details in the figure. However,
the simple observation of the figs. 62 a) and 62 b) shows that certain

116

details, for example FG and F'G' are slightly different and produce angles with slightly different power which causes one to contract first and the other to contract after, forming different contractions at least in that detail. This difference will then be absorbed in the following contraction. Also from my experience I know that the comparison between the umpteenth contraction of the current form and the umpteenth contraction of the memorized form is often incomplete, it is better to extend the comparison between the layer n of the current figure between the layers n+i and n-i (i=1,2,3,...) because in this way the detail that disappeared in the layer n reappears in the nearby layer of depth. The three criteria listed before for finding corresponding angles remain valid. Another advantage of this position is that with it the algorithm accepts more easily the disproportions of the figure. Think of the profile of a man in fig. 60 a) but that the man has a much bigger chin and a much smaller forehead than the one in fig. 60 b). The comparison of layer n of the current figure with the layer n of the memorized figure would not function. If i is small, i=2 or i=3 on a total of twenty layers, the small disproportions will be absorbed while the big ones, which would impede a child from defining the two figures as similar, remain irreconcilable. The disproportionate zones will be detected because they have no connections and treated with the method of syntactic recognition.

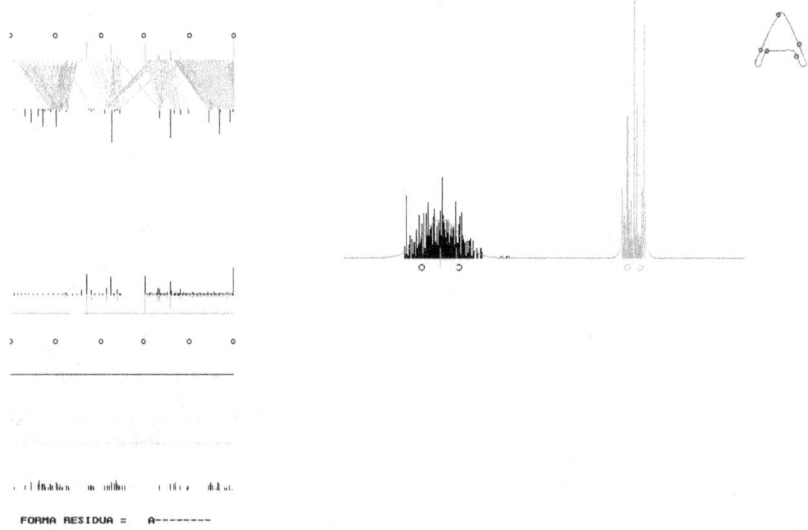

Fig. 62

On the computer I have implemented programmes based on these ideas and their result is visible in fig. 62 a) in which two forms of fig 65 are compared, one in the upper left and one in the lower left. The first in the upper left in fig 65 is the memorized form which in the programme is called "residual form" and in the following paragraph the reason for this will be clear. It has been given the name A----- which defines a class of similar forms. The first on the lower left of fig. 65 is the current form and its "silhouette" is visible in fig. 62 in the upper right. On this there are small circles that divide the perimeter in five parts. The perimeter of the current form is developed on the upper side of the "rectangle", through light grey and dark grey lines (red and green on the internet site), that are in the upper left in fig 62. The six small circles divide it into five parts, like the silhouette. The small circles are six because the first and the last refer to coincident elements. The first small circle is in the highest point on the left of the silhouette and goes in a clockwise direction. Instead in the lower side of the rectangle there is the development of the perimeter of the residual form. The vertical lines (green), normally on the upper side of the rectangle represent the power of the angles of contracted lines of the current figure. The vertical lines (yellow), normally on the lower side are instead the power of the angles of the contracted lines of the residual form. The dark grey lines (green) between the lower and upper sides of the rectangle represent all the possible connections, the light grey ones (red) the corrected connections. Notice that all the angles are connected by a light grey line (red) despite the fact that the figures are very different. This is because the contractions make the contracted lines of the current form and the residual form equal, at least from a certain contracted line down. An algorithm makes it possible to calculate the power satisfied by the connections, to then use this information as criteria for establishing to which class the form belongs. For example, if the residual forms were around one hundred, the current figure would be confronted with them all and with every confrontation the satisfaction of the angles would be expressed by a number. If all goes well the maximum of these numbers would correspond to the residual form with the name A----- and the current form would be recognised in this class, therefore it would have the name A-----.

Notice that the silhouette of the residual form does not appear because its angles, its sides are the result of the workings of a neuronal network which eliminates a part, which makes averages. This representation makes the design of the residual form laboured and difficult. Indeed if the high contracted lines are not conserved it is impossible. So it is for humans: recognising an object does not mean knowing how to draw it.

4. The neuronal network. Fragmentation of the figure.

While testing my ideas on the computer, I wrote a programme which simulated a classical neuronal network. Nothing exceptional. This made averages between similar figures, the distances between vertexes, the bisectors, the values of the angles, the depth of the layer of the angle in question and attributed a persistence to the angle. Persistence is a characteristic that is different from power. The power of an angle depends on its acumen and the length of its sides, independently of the number of times in which it occurs. Persistence makes it possible to cancel an angle, if it is relatively little in respect to the number of times the figure has been seen and recognised, furthermore normalized persistence in respect of the number of times that the figure has been seen and recognised supplies further criteria to define the connection between the angles of the current form and the memorized form. I called "residual form" the memorized form, refined by averages with a consequential strengthening of the persistence of the angles and their cancellation. From tests it came out that for topological recognition the neuronal network didn't do much good. The forms were recognised with the same probability of error both after one form was shown to the computer and memorized and when many were memorized and an average made. However, the neuronal network is not useless, it gives the possibility to 1) define the type of intelligence 2) close edges 3) fragment an image. These are its workings, homonymy apart, we attribute the same name to a figure which we judge to be similar. We limit the meaning of this word to what a child, less than three years old, would give to it. At the beginning many different figures show up on the computer, each one with its own name and we ask it to memorize them with their names. After this if I want the computer to recognise a figure (the current figure), I present it to its visual apparatus, it extracts the configuration, it compares it with the figures already memorized which have a name, finds the one most similar to it and gives it its name. This is recognition; it takes place between the current configuration and the residual one and there are elements that correspond and others that don't. The distance of the elements from their origin, the bisectors, the position of the contracted lines in the layers, the powers are all averaged with a weighted average, taking into consideration how many times the figure with that name has appeared and the result of such averages is to correct the data which are in the residual form. The length of the elements that do not correspond are varied in order to preserve the previous order of the elements. A,B,C,D,E are the vertexes of a contracted line and only B and E find correspondence with the current contracted line, because of this B and E come closer together. The order of the vertexes after this operation still remains A,B,C,D,E even if B and E have come closer, so much as to over-ride the primitive positions of C and D. The displacement of B and E brings about the displacement of all the points, also the ones that do not correspond. Imagine the development of the polygonal on an elastic, pulling apart or nearing B and E, the other points move but their order remains the same. In detail the displacements will be more or less large in relation to the power and persistence of the elements that correspond or do not correspond. Regarding the bisectors, those of the corresponding angles are averaged with a weighted average. The privileged difference is found for the others then these bisectors are increased by this difference taking into account that also the increase is subject to the weighted average. Regarding the persistence of the corresponding elements, it is increased every time the form is recognised. The number of times the form has been presented is also taken into account and the relationship between them and the number of times the form has been presented is more important than the persistence. This relationship which I call relative persistence p, multiplied by the power P affects the calculation of the numerical

121

value which measures similarity. The increase of persistence is different for every layer of the configuration and makes it possible to define the type of intelligence of the machine. A great increase for high contracted lines, elaborated little, involves a very precise type of intelligence, unable to generalize, which it consider to be similar only in figures that are almost identical. If then the approximations on the angles, on the bisectors and on the lengths were minimum, the knowledge of a restricted environment would require an enormous quantity of memory in order to register a large number of almost identical forms. On the contrary, if I greatly increase the low contracted lines, I would distinguish badly because too many forms produce the same high contracted lines. Common sense says it is better to define a function that privileges the intermediate contracted lines or to study one suitable to a purpose, a position that clashes with the assumptions of the general work. There are zones of the perimeter of the residual contracted lines without any element. These zones accept elements from the same zone as the current contracted line. There are psychological studies which show how a newborn baby forms the mother's face in his mind, its outlines are prolonged day by day until they are completed, as in fig. 63. I have noted that the first outlines that form in the baby, like in the machine, are those that have the highest gradient, and are therefore the easiest to detect. Relative persistence makes it possible to identify the elements of the residual contracted lines that can be cancelled. It is enough to impose that if, after n times that the form has been recognised, there are elements with a low p. If in a zone of the outline there are angles that normally have values very different from the residual figure, they are weakened and are cancelled but those of the current figure, also different, cannot become stable and the result is a void in that zone of the outline. Since I was young I have called these parts of the outline articular zones, referring to the articulation of the human body. They are in figs. 64 a) and b). The zones A,B and A',B' where the variation of the angle cannot be absorbed by a reasonable approximation.

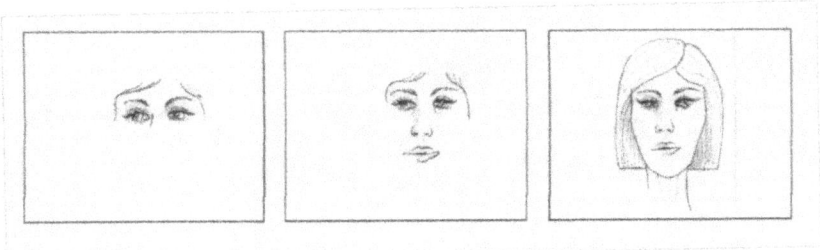

Fig. 63

What I have said for the right arm applies to the left and, in general, also for the legs, even if it is evident in the figs. 64 a) and b), furthermore it applies also for the forearm and elbow… In general where there is an articulation the angles are so different that the angle registered after the first perception is not recognised as the same anymore in the successive one and its low persistence causes it to be cancelled: in this zone the memorized outline of the figure breaks down. The neuronal network, united with the definition I have given of the characteristics, provokes something similar to what I had expected in a completely different context, Marr wanted to break down the figure into pieces as in fig.64 c). The fragmentation takes place thanks to movement. I repeat that I don't have the energy or the capacity to carry out alone studies on objects in movement. Each one of these figures which take form can have a name and are connected to each other through eye movement and other changes in the cerebral state.

123

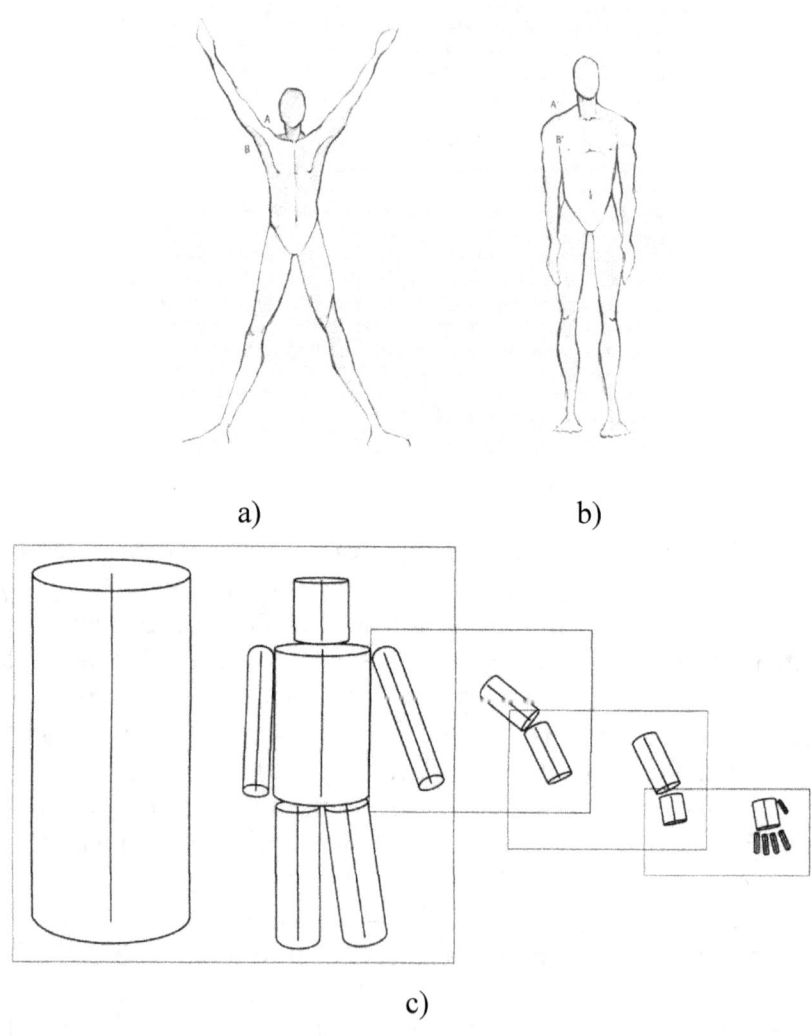

a)

b)

c)

Figs. 64

124

The case of a three-dimensional figure, for example a human face, is different, it gives at least two different images if seen from the front or in profile and these are memorized as different forms. (under the same name). If the face, seen from the front, turns a little towards the profile view, the angles that describe it remain roughly equal and it is recognised but if the face is sharply in profile its angles are completely different from those seen from the front, therefore more than two memorizations are necessary for following the rotation of the figure. Also here I don't agree with Marr, in my opinion the forms in the brain have a bidimensional structure. The case of a figure which is seen very frequently with its details disposed in a certain way and rarely in another position is different again, as if the man in the figure were seen almost always with his arms at his sides. In this case the outline does not break but diversity is detected and makes it possible to isolate the same part which is in an unusual position. This fragmentation is the base of syntactic recognition. The parts of the outline that are void are not like those that have not yet formed, where there is contrast but it is weak: in these parts the angles are always equal and we witness their strengthening. The problem of the fragmentation of the object can be treated in the same way as that of the revelation of differences between similar objects. The differences are very important for distinguishing forms. It can happen that two similar forms are confused because the detail that would permit them to be distinguished in topological recognition has little weight in the calculation that establishes similarity between forms. If, for example, O and Q are the two forms to be recognised, the tail of the Q could be seen as an insignificant disturbance and the forms would be confused. This will not happen if the tail is isolated and memorized as the element that discriminates between the two forms. From these words one senses that the recognition of Q or O requires two distinct perceptions, that of the circle and that of the tail, that can be there and must be in a certain zone or be missing. This is an example of syntactic recognition of which I will talk further. Teaching the machine can be done through a teacher who can indicate the tail and explain that in order to understand if the letter is an O or a Q the machine must check that the tail is there or not, as a child would do. However, the work of a teacher is not the only way to learn, an intelligent child is able to isolate the discriminating difference on his own. I have developed some programmes for this which, differently from those of movement, are within my power. They make it possible to isolate the details that are different between the two forms and, for other purposes, would pick out also the articular zones. The core is the programme up to now applied for recognising forms, adapted for two forms which tend to be confused. It picks out and indicates the part that is different between the two similar forms, it isolates it and memorizes it. As an example the reader asks what is the principal difference between the letters A and R, drawn in the figs. 65 and 56.

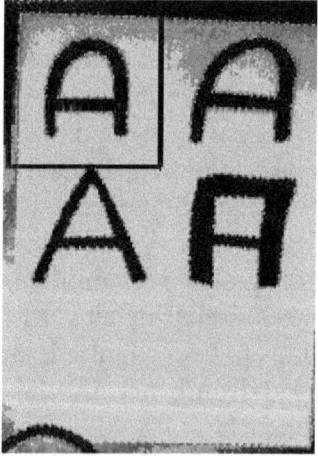

Fig. 65
He will read no further because the answer is in his mind. The letters A and R are quite similar and anyone would agree that the

fundamental difference lies in the recess in the middle if R on its right side. If the computer could locate it we could be sure that it functioned like a human. In fig. 66 there is the result of a comparison between the residual form of A, called A------- and the first R at the top on the left of fig. 55, which is the current form and is drawn in fig. 66 at the top on the right. At the top on the left in fig. 66 in the "rectangle" the connection between the contracted lines of A and R are shown in light grey (red). The angles of the perimeter of the form R are arranged on the upper side of the rectangle. Starting from the point on the top on the left of the silhouette of R and continuing clockwise its recess falls between the second and third small circle. Looking at the upper side of the rectangle in question, that of the current form of R, enlarged in fig. 67 between the second and third small circle, the predominance of dark grey (green) which indicates the angles, is noticeable, they cannot be connected in a valid way to the residual form of A, represented on the lower side. They are the angles of the recess of R. It is also noticeable that in correspondance with the fourth small circle there is a zone that is not connected which corresponds to the bifurcation between the legs of the R. In fact the disproportion between this detail of R and the width of the segment which connects the two legs of A is too great to be absorbed. Repeating the comparison between the various A and R of different shapes the two isolating details will be refined by the neuronal network. The first will certainly be conserved and in the definition of the recognition of A with respect to R it will be essential, the second detail could disappear or have less weight.

Obviously the weight can be mechanized because it is defined by persistence. If the figures that are compared with this programme were not A and R but rather the forms of figs. 63, immediately the machine would isolate the two arms, which could be memorized with a specific programme, the same which is used to memorize the recess in R.

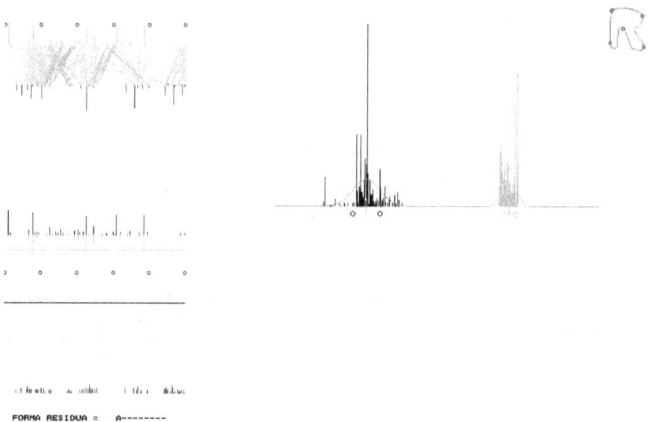

Fig 66

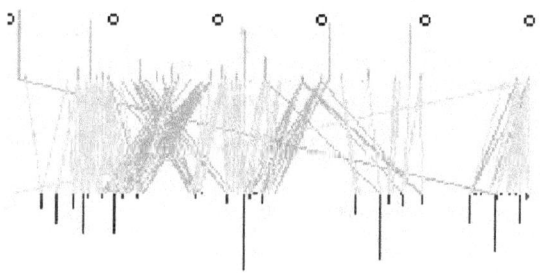

Fig. 67

Topological recognition supplies values that quantify the similarity between the current form and the various residual forms, one for each residual form. The highest value associates the name of the residual figure with the current figure. Every residual figure has a name which has been assigned to it. The current figure no. The computer must understand to which residual figure it is similar and attribute its name to it. If the highest value that emerges from the comparison

128

between the current figure and the residual one differs little from the successive value, it can be said that the topological recognition is doubtful and it is necessary to proceed to the syntactic one, If, instead, a value is much greater than the others (these words must be specified with a percentage) there is no sense in proceeding with the syntactic recognition. The topological recognition is already sure.

5. Notes on the search for objects

Limiting ourselves only to vision, objects are isolated in the environment because of 1) movement and above all 2) the variation of movement. In these conditions they attract attention. The first cause is easily mechanized, it is enough to consider two images of the same scene in temporal succession and the image of the object in motion appears from their difference. Even if the eye moves on a uniform background, for example a lovely green field, with this technique an immobile piece of wastepaper can be isolated. A uniform movement is ignored after a short time too. This behaviour is also proper to the other senses as well as to sight, for example, despite the fact that all the weight of the body is on our feet, we don't feel the pressure on them. In both cases the object is brought to the central vision, scaled and its characteristics are extracted in order to be recognised. However, an object, also immobile and quite indistinguishable on a varied background, can also be found. It is for this purpose that animals use their sense of smell a lot. Wanting to use only sight I remember that I have already shown the similarity between the plane model of the retina and the layered model and that an image in a deep plane corresponds "more or less" to an image elaborated on a deep layer. The plane model and the layered model are two applications of convergence, which is a characteristic of the visual system. If you want, for example, to find a house in a

129

landscape of cars, trees, animals, you can stimulate the residual configuration of the house and look at the landscape with the peripheral vision method. The house occupies a minimal area in the visual circle which is a large circle, suited to peripheral vision. Given the high convergence of the optic fibres on the same visual nerve the house cannot contain details. It will be elaborated (like the rest of the image) in the layered model and its high contracted lines will find correspondance in the low ones, memorized, of the house. This is because the residual form derives from the observation of the house in central vision, the high contracted lines which proceed from the central vision cannot find confirmation with the high ones which derive from peripheral vision, which derive from an image with few details. The high contracted lines of the peripheral vision find confirmation in the lower contracted lines of the residual form, in which the details of the house have been eliminated with another method but with similar results. Because of this correspondence the house can be isolated in central vision in order to be recognised with certainty.

6. The structure of the visual cells

The cell of visual memory that I have created on the computer is very simple. It consists of a configuration, that is, a set of contracted lines, a name and any possible synonyms. In the cerebral model which I propose, in general the memory cells, not only the visual ones, are more complex, schematized in fig. 68. Their characteristics are found in the last line, which for the visual system are in the configuration. In the first line they have an index i which is the cardinal number of the cell. Then they have a memorizing zone formed by some lines. In it a, b, ..., e, f, ...are the indexes of other brain cells, there is the power p_i, calculated based on the frequency with which the memorization of the index repeats

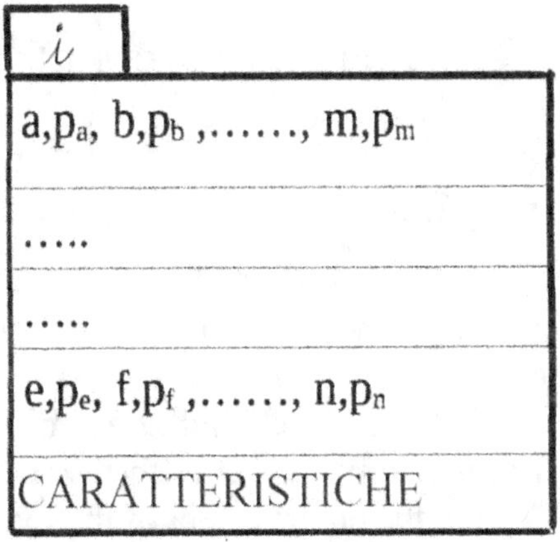

i		
$a,p_a,\ b,p_b\ ,\ldots\ldots,\ m,p_m$		
$\ldots\ldots$		
$\ldots\ldots$		
$e,p_e,\ f,p_f\ ,\ldots\ldots,\ n,p_n$		
CARATTERISTICHE		

fig. 68

I would like to point out that in the memory zone of a cell the indexes of every type of cell in the brain can be memorized, therefore, for example, a cell of the visual system can contain in its memory indexes of both the auditory system and the visual system. It is not so on the line of characteristics: the cells of the visual system contain the characteristics of vision, that is configurations: the cells of the auditory system have in their lines characteristics that belong to the auditory system, etc... Once the set of cells relative to a sense were called levels and also those of control inside the brain. It can be said that summoning the characteristics of a cell produces stimulation in it but its stimulation can also be induced by the summons of its index. In due ways a stimulated cell can memorize and emit what it has memorized.

131

Chapter VI – The mechanization of language

Preliminary remarks

The connection between the world and the brain is assured, with many limits, by the senses. This evolutionary effort does not seem to have developed in order to know self and its essence but to satisfy instinctive needs. The predictive power of the brain has developed within these limits and in the environment of the living. In my opinion the evolutionary process of the brain started from a protozoan membrane which let nutritional liquids enter and kept poisonous ones out. Then the amoeba which wrapped itself around a microscopic being and "tasted" it before absorbing it, using a rudimental chemiosensorial apparatus, which evaluated the molecules from which its prey was formed. An apparatus which remained partly the same and partly transformed into something similar to the sense of smell, which captured the molecules scattered by the prey in the water and then in the air. The sense of sight came after, from the necessity to avoid obstacles and proceed in a rough environment and also the need to locate prey or predators which, however, were still recognised by their smell. Only in superior animals and man, to which I will refer in the following presentation, the sense of sight acquires the capacity to recognise objects. To this end the eye captures photons which are emanations of the world, as are the molecules which concern the chemiosensorial apparatus. The eye, stimulated by photons, emits electric discharges which are elaborated and take information content to the brain. The elaboration partly brings about vision which permits humans to orientate and

132

partly permits the recognition of objects. The recognition of objects, actioned by the sense of sight, which is based on photons, is much more efficient for the complex needs of humans than that operated by the chemiosensorial apparatus. The information carried by these signals which have predictive power, give sense to the word "models of the mind", acceptable with this definition, even if they derive from language and ways of describing that are not mine. The cerebral model depends on how the information that reaches the brain from the sense is elaborated but also from the emanation that the sense detects. A model derived from sounds, which are vibrations is different from one derived from smells and different again from one derived from photons. They are different representations of the world, those which have developed more or less, which have specialized in the process of natural selection. For about one hundred years there has been a general aversion towards models. Some respected professors of physics define models as "the help of weak minds" other professors of physics say, en passant (sic!), instead of starting a detailed discussion that models must be avoided because a) they have shown their limits in the 1920s with the study of atomic physics and continue saying b) a physics theory is good when from a series of measurements another series can be anticipated and measured. This second claim b) is true but futile, inconsistent, superficial. It has the same limits as the classic relation cause and effect that is inherent in the predictive model formed by evolution. It is the result of natural selection which, through the extermination of those who could not adapt, has made the senses and the brain able to establish this relationship through the choice made by the brain of the opportune emanations of the world and the elaboration of sensorial signals that they produce. For example, in the game of billiards there is an excellent predictive model and, in fact, billiard champions, who usually have not carried out studies on rational mechanics, know how to predict the trajectories of the balls in an excellent way. Probably this game and anyway the cerebral model has given a noticeable contribution to the discovery of the mathematical formulation of the law of conservation of the quantity of motion that permits, united with that of the conservation of energy, to know the position and speed of the balls after impacts and rebounds. This is a model of vision, linked to photons and the information that they carry. There is no sense in exploring the atomic and subatomic world with photons, that matter interferes and reacts with them in an unpredictable way. The photon cannot be compared to a bull in a china shop as a famous physicist said. If it were so, the damage caused by the beast would be comprehensible. Furthermore in atomic physics the word velocity, the word position and the intuitive idea of matter itself lose their sense, confusing themselves with the waves. Essentially no one knows what is being talked about and it is not known how the object being studied behaves, it is not known how it evolves. How is it possible to formulate laws in mathematical form if it is not understood what is happening? There is no predictive model in itself, like there is in the billiards game, on which to lay down a form of mathematics that makes it possible to refine and quantify predictions already in place. It must never be forgotten that mathematics is a mere tautology. Furthermore in order to quantify it is necessary to measure. In the atomic and subatomic world what is measured? No one knows what is being talked about. It is not possible to apply to that world the model that we have in mind, the model that we have obtained from photons, we might as well try to apply it to that which derives from smells or from sounds. It would take new senses that discover appropriate emanations of that world and a brain organized in a way to form a predictive model. Only evolution can do this, then a theory in mathematical form can be written. Most physicists, my contemporaries, instead, go backwards. They try to apply to that world laws in mathematical form, which have been obtained from the macroscopic world, not thinking that they are relationships within a

134

cerebral model of that environment that as a base has photons and therefore carries information from the world that it can give. It is not as if I can do better: simply I can't stubbornly go on with an impossible enterprise and, since no one knows how the microscopic world is, neither do I propose to design senses in the brain to understand it. It would take repeated attempts, simulating natural selection. Unfortunately, in my opinion, these considerations lead to the impossibility of any progress in understanding the microcosm. Discoveries may come from increasingly powerful machines, which will give rise to theories that are only partial and of little predictive power. Indeed these theories will be continually amended by further experimental discoveries. I have not changed these ideas since I was twenty-one, twenty-two years old and they further convinced me to continue with my studies of the brain and give secondary importance to the studies of physics as conceived today, with a certain regret because I had glimpsed shattering implications in the relativistic extension of thermology, but this is not the main reason: for brain studies I renounced politics, this is my great regret. However, the brain is also a physical organ and the study of physics concerns every natural thing, not just elementary particles or the theory of relativity. What I did, for what it is worth, is a work of classical physics because the brain I designed lies within the macrocosm, the world we know with the senses, made of things that move, that give heat, that make noise, etc..., of which the brain has made itself a model that has a strong predictive power. The measures and mathematics that connect them make sense because they concern measurable quantities in the sense given by Euclid to these words and are methods that serve exclusively to perfect the predictive power inherent in the model. In the typical superabundance of the brain model, choosing the parts, or signs if you prefer, useful for predicting can be perfected using quantitative methods and demanding exact previsions from a quantitative point of view, writing the theory in mathematical form. Mathematics in physics is subordinate to the model but adds nothing to it. Logic is then a support for mathematics. It is not true that models must be avoided because they have demonstrated their limits in the 1920s with the study of atomic physics. Physics stopped there in those years because it had no brain model to make forecast, to mathematize. I agree with David Hume, the law of physics is a habit. The relationship cause and effect is another way to name the habit. Nothing is further from me than the Platonic conception, accepted by Galileo, of a world made of proportions and geometric figures. We know nothing of anything, to each one the opinion comes from without. There is nothing to add to these words of the great Democritus.

I must now take up the initial discourse, that is of the cerebral state A which anticipates , through the cerebral state B the evolution of the physical state X towards the physical state Y which generates B. Naturally the environmental state Y must be important for the living. Note that almost always the cerebral state A is composed of two objects: A' called agent and P called patient. A' provokes the transformation of P in P'. It is always true that A is followed by B but A must be seen as A'+P and B is seen normally as A'+P'. The presence of a cause of the transformation is so usual that it is part of the way of thinking of children who, when something happens, immediately try to find out "who did it". Furthermore in humans but also in animals, the cause of transformation attracts attention through neurophysiological devices, which act automatically on the variation of stimulation. Therefore the primitive definition, while remaining legitimate, should be adapted to this cerebral operation. The agent makes it possible to predict whether and how the patient will evolve into a final state. For example the situation A is composed of two objects: one is in the form of cheese, the other a mouse. If the mouse\ (agent) comes closer to the cheese (patient) it can be expected that the latter will be diminished and nibbled, that is transformed. In order

136

to reach the prevision the brain distinguishes an agent and a patient in the situation X: what is important is the transformation of the patient, from this derive benefits or damage. The reflection of this process should be found in natural language, it should be clear who carries out the action and who is subjected to it, transforming, which is the most important fact. In fact more and more evidence is being found that in ancient languages the agent and the patient had essential roles and were recognisable either by the way in which the sentence is formed or by a suffix,... These languages are said to be ergative and they are the direct result of attentional mechanisms, of the necessity of the brain to predict. In the indoeuropean languages, not only the modern ones but also in Latin, ancient Greek, ancient Slavic,... the ergative case has disappeared but some traces remain which cause us to presume (for the competent) that ancient protoindoeuropean was an ergative language. Ergative languages, despite a sharp decline, have not disappeared completely, an example in Europe there is Basque, as well as some Caucasian languages. In my opinion these languages, exactly because they are ancient, were nearer to the cerebral function than modern languages, even if it has been demonstrated, with neurophysiological experience that the brain activity for formulating thoughts in ergative languages was greater and therefore more difficult than in the languages that do not have this case. Probably it was a question of reducing this effort that has brought about their death throes. In a hypothetical English where the agent and the patient are prominent, for example, with the final A for agent and the final P for patient the phrase the mouse eats the cheese would have the form: the mouseA (agent) eats the cheeseP (patient). It is crucial to note that in such a language the subject of the intransitive verb is treated as the patient of the transitive verb. In the phrase the pot (subject) bursts (intransitive verb in active form) it would become in the hypothetical English: potP bursts. It would be very clear that the pot is subjected to the action. In English, a language that is substantially nominative-accusative, for logical analysis the pot is the subject and with the active verb the subject carries out the action. Here the bursting pot is on the receiving end of the action, therefore substantially the pot is the object! There would not be this confusion in an ergative language, it is always clear who/what is the patient. This reflection of brain activity on language confirms that for the brain, the patient is important, the one who is subjected to the action and is transformed into something which could be useful, harmful or not worthy of note. Another proof of the importance of the patient in ancient languages and therefore in brain activity comes from Basque. As in the non-ergative languages the role of the patient and the agent is evident only in the passive form, the Basque people, excluding the élite, not having yet a clear idea of the nature of their language, to explain it to foreigners, said that it was a strange language where verbs had only the passive form. Despite their error even they, who had not studied linguistics, had noted that their language gave importance to the patient. The agent is important for predicting the type of transformation, for making hypothesis about it, it is not important in itself.

However not all verbs express an action, in particular the verb 'to be' is used to describe a situation in the relationship between its parts, without any action whatsoever. It is substantially different from other verbs and, in fact in certain languages, like Arab, this verb is not present. Both the agent and the patient, before or after the transformation can be objects formed by objects that are spatially related to each other. The verb clarifies the agent, it tells us how it acts, when it will act, with what probability. In natural language it is, however,something difficult to subject to rules worthy of the name or operational definitions and the grammar books I have read to throw light on the mechanization of language have only been a source of frustration. Frustration that was not only mine, I remember that the attempt to create automatic translation using only grammatical analysis carried out through a computer programme called 'parsing' that , within its modest limits, carried out one or another formal grammar, was a failure. Always concerning languages it was certainly the observation of our ancestors that an object can appear alone or in more copies, it can belong or not to the one who is speaking, it can be inside or outside other objects,.. to develop and express in language concepts of plurality, appearance, inclusion,... they are frequent cases associated with any object which the language must express economically, not defining different words for each of these states. In English the plural form is normally formed by adding an 's' to the singular, tooth and teeth are a rare exception, but imagine if every plural were irregular. In almost all languages there are roots of words to which are added affixes (which can be suffixes, infixes or prefixes) to explain recurring situations or to explain the grammatical function of the word. Also in the French and Italian languages there are singular and plural cases, masculine and feminine,... Also for the consequences of actions the process was similar and, in fact, verbs have tenses and modes to express when the action will take place, if its result will be sure, how long it will last,.. but there are languages that take this procedure to extremes, that have a high number of affixes and make great use of them and tend to be very regular. One of these languages is Japanese which has only one irregular verb. They are called agglutinatived (a term which derives from Latin and means to glue). Sumerian was both an agglutinative language and an ergative one. However, in my opinion, the agglutination of a language is not such an interesting phenomenon like ergativity, because it can be explained with mere economical considerations, with different attempts by every speaking community, not so directly tied to brain function. The economic motives are not only of the community but also of the speaker when he constructs a sentence, in which he combines the names of objects in a personal way. The English language which, at the moment, is the best known language in the world, is losing its verb endings and is going towards maintaining only the roots of words. Languages of this type are called isolating languages, Chinese is amongst them so isolating languages are not rare!

The brain, the organ dedicated to predicting and language expands this function, vastly improving the possibility of the transmission of knowledge through teaching. In inferior animals, knowledge is transferred almost entirely in their genes, gradually as the evolutionary scale is climbed, this is always less true and the only innate knowledge of humans is to suck their mother's breast, everything else must be learned. Moreover structural language, through sentences, makes it possible to fragment the redundant visual perception by isolating and enhancing the elements which are useful for prediction, perhaps minimal, neglecting the rest which would lead to considering useful elements as an irrelevant disturbance. This makes it possible to teach the recognition of important situations with precision, not only through a single perception, but describable through objects known to the learner and also to specify which are the details to be considered crucial in that situation, which make it possible to distinguish it from similar situations. It is obvious that this requires a store of previous memories common to the teacher and the student. Without previous knowledge, learning through language is impossible.

In the following pages I will not consider the sense of hearing in its capacity of exploring the world but solely as a receptor of language implemented by a speaker. Language that will be considered as formed by a series of signs, without ambiguity, that are associated with perceptions not of all the senses, as would be logical, but only visual perceptions and changes in cerebral states. The reader could easily generalize. The title of the book itself leaves no doubts and it will be considered that language derives from the mechanistic function of the brain, in particular of a conceptual apparatus that can be created which I will call control device, of which, I am sorry to say, I have no neurophysiological evidence. Such a device, foreseen also by Chomsky, should allow, in the first instance, the comparison between visual images formed from only one perception and the corresponding memorized image to establish with what probability they are equal or different and proceed to another cerebral operation, that could be a call to perform an action. This procedure is identical also for animals. However, humans possess a structured language and therefore the control device should control the correspondence between an image composed of details placed in certain positions and having certain dimensions,... it is a sentence. This happens with commands that make the eyes move, that focus them, etc., These atomic commands can be grouped and memorized in just one word or with different words and this can happen in very different ways permitting a great deal of grammar to form. The control device carries out these atomic commands in sequence, in an orderly way, but sometimes not in the same order as they are contained in the word or the sentence, because one of the essential tasks of the control device is that of putting in order the controls so that the same controls on the visual image can be generated with different sentences. Every language, but partly every speaker, groups together the criteria that are absolutely unpredictable, variable and generate different sentences for describing the same image. Rather than analysing in detail how the link between sentence and image is formed through logical-mathematical formulas. I consider it important to describe operationally the devices whose function is such as to produce this brain function. For this new hypothesis are needed but dictated by good sense. For example, if the human eye is made to look up, making it follow the movement of a rising finger, it has sense to think that there is an apparatus that emits impulses that go to the eye muscles and make it rotate in the appropriate direction. At the same time the word "up" can be pronounced which memorizes these impulses, which referring to a single device, I will call atomic impulses. The eye looks up if these impulses reach it, both if they come from this apparatus, but also as a result of the emission of the same memorized impulses, for example, in the word "up". Naturally there is an unconscious and automatic attentional process which attracts the eye to the moving finger. The eye focuses and follows it but what is of interest now are the impulses that make it rotate. The reader can easily generalize and adapt the argument to a device constructed by him but the forced rotation of the eye will always take place by sending appropriate impulses to the actuators, which can be memorized . Every device including the control device can be induced by impulses to perform an operation. If, for example, they are memorized in a word, which emits them when the word is pronounced, the device will repeat that action. A sentence could also be controlled in the memory and not only about the world. It is an argument that I have still to develop. However, up to now I can conclude that the various grammars of natural languages cannot be reduced to mathematical logic, to formal systems: a sentence is not a well constructed formula, it is tied to the function of the senses and the control device, which leave space to incompleteness and contradictions for which humans find remedies with previous knowledge. Finally I would like to make it clear that I have not carried out experiments on the mechanization of language due to the lack of an apparatus that can be connected to the world and of my ability to build one. What follows therefore has hypothetical value.

1. Voice recognition

Usually in grammar books we read that phonemes are the smallest units of sound that allow us to form the words of a language. Instead graphemes or letters are signs to represent sounds. Constructing a machine that transforms a phoneme into a grapheme means recognising that a sound is a certain vowel or a certain consonant. This is difficult and at the moment it is a conceptually unsolved problem (I say conceptually because systems of voice recognition exist and function quite well, if not very well). At the moment (2017) as far as I know, in order to recognise graphemes in phonemes, the acoustic wave which comes out of the mouth is taken and it is transformed with a microphone into an electric signal, which depends on the intensity of the pressure of the sound wave in time. It is fractioned into temporal segments, widely overlapping and it is supposed that each one of these fractions of wave (of brief duration, only a few hundredths of a second) constitutes the sum of sinusoidal waves of different amplitude and frequency, obtained with numerical calculation procedures based on a nineteenth-century mathematical formula of Fourier. These sinusoid sums are called spectrums and it is customary to form diagrams having the frequencies on the abscissa and their amplitudes on the ordinate. Unfortunately one notices that the spectrum of the same phoneme is different depending on the speaker and the word in which it is inserted. This observation is very true for consonants, perhaps a little too severe for vowels. An interesting conceptual study should look for characteristics which remain constant for each phoneme, instead it is preferred to memorize their spectrums. In this way excellent practical results are obtained, due to heuristics, supported by the power of modern calculators. The reader who is interested in the argument should understand clearly mathematical representation and in particular the fast Fourier transform, which speeds up calculations and something on the model of Markov, for the calculation of probability. Briefly, a system of voice recognition for commercial use works like this (in the year 2017): at the training stage it memorizes very many frequency spectrums for every phoneme, which derive from different ways of speaking, and a content of different words. Furthermore the system memorizes statistical data such as the probability that a phoneme is in a certain spectrum. At the end of the comparisons the system recognises, that is, it associates a grapheme to a phoneme, based on the maximum probability of its spectrum components. Finally, having recognised the phonemes probabilistically the word must be in the vocabulary of the predefined language and also in the context of conversation, absolutely undefinable but also delimited by heuristics. I have not explained the choice of the transformation of the signal in a frequency spectrum, also because these are calculated on such a small temporal segment. I have limited myself to referring. I am far from this way of working, not that I don't know how to do better or not even that I have tried because I have always concentrated on vision where I found the invariant forms in the angles and developed this idea. This is because above all it is with the eye that humans are in contact with the external world and the predictive model is formed. Hearing has less importance for knowing the world and I have not wanted or been able to spend efforts and energy studying a secondary objective. Within the limits that I imposed upon myself the hearing system has only linguistic use. I might as well eliminate it and pass on to the the written word with typographical characters of unequivocal recognition. Therefore I consider for my purpose the problem is resolved. I will call my device a decoder.

2. The structure of the linguistic area of the brain

With the term phoneme I mean that a codification has the same information content as a grapheme, that is, let's suppose that pronouncing the letter 'n' the same phoneme is produced, independently from its position in a word, from the sound wave that generates it and from the spectrum that can be derived from it. There is a limited number of phonemes each one of which has its own index, that is, a cardinal number. If desired, they can be thought of as decoder outputs. In the brain model that I propose, I assume that hearing is limited to receiving the spoken word and to derive the phonemes that another person pronounces. I have said that the problem is practically resolved with commercial apparatus for recognising speech. I have not gone into the question because for my purposes the grapheme, which would have the same function, could be inserted with a keyboard. The passage from the phoneme index to its vocal pronunciation is possible and has been resolved much more easily than the reverse process. Obviously one must not expect the diction of an actor. The linguistic area of the brain is composed of cells like those in fig. 68, placed on a hierarchical scale. The lowest plane, which is 0, corresponds with the phoneme cells. Each phoneme has its cell and the content line of characteristics is pre-established and immutable. The indexes of the phoneme cells, grouped in an arbitrary way, constitute the content of the line of the characteristics of the syllable cells and the syllable cells form plane 1. The indexes of the syllable cells, grouped in an arbitrary way, constitute the content of the line of the word cells and the word cells form plane 2. The indexes of the word cells, grouped in an arbitrary way, constitute the content of the line of the characteristics of the sentence cells and the sentence cells form plane 3, etc..etc... These names have been chosen in analogy with those used in grammar books. Excluding the phoneme cells, which have a predetermined line of characteristics and can be thought to be connected with the decoder, the other cells have the line of characteristics initially empty, and it can hold only a limited number of elements. These hypothesis derive from the observation that in human language there are not long words. The characteristics of the cells of the auditory system can be written as:

$$a, p_a, \; b, p_b \;, \ldots\ldots\ldots, \; n, p_n \qquad (3)$$

$a, b, \ldots, n$ represents the index of a cell in the auditory system and $p_b, \ldots\ldots, p_n$ the persistences of this index. The auditory level has a hierarchical structure because the cells of the top layer can have only the indexes of the cells of the lower layer in the characteristics line. Sequences of analogous indexes and those of (3) are preserved in the memorization lines of the cell. However, the indexes are not those of the auditory system but indexes of any level of the brain and any plane of the auditory level. I would like to point out the substantial difference between planes of the auditory level and the layers of the visual level. In the visual level the layer derives from the contraction of the elements of the lower level and therefore the top contracted line represents a generalization of the lower one. In the visual level the layers are all in just one cell, each one of them contains a contracted line, together they form the configuration and are its characteristics. In the auditory level the top plane is formed by cells whose characteristics are a collection of indexes of the cells of the lower level. This collection does not occur based on an algorithm, but in principle can be unpredictable, there is no generalization intent in passing from a word to a sentence. I would also like to point out that (3) has a beginning and an end. For example, leaving out the persistences, if the characteristics of a word cell are: 12, 47, 52, 19 they refer to a specific cell, different from the cell which has the characteristics 45, 12, 47, 52, 19, 66, even if this succession includes the previous one. When the speaker must teach a word he pronounces it, separating it from the others with a long temporal pause, instead, when the line of characteristics is memorized, the pauses will not be very important any more. The pauses, apart from being indispensable for words, serve to define the sentences and periods, instead it seems that nature has provided for syllables as they correspond to

146

increasing sound intensity which ceases quite abruptly to give place to the increase in intensity of the next syllable.

3. Spontaneous and stimulated emissions

Molecules, electrical impulses, synapses etc.. circulate in the biological brain and the transmission of information takes place with them. In computers there are electrical impulses. In a text like this one, of a general character, it is not necessary to specify the physical support of the information. It is enough to say, for example, the address cell i is excited when the information referring to the address i circulates in the brain or the information that recalls the characteristics contained in the characteristics zone of the cell circulates. Such information can be emitted by a cell, from the senses or a device suitable for the purpose. For example, the cell in fig. 68 can always generate an emission from its memory zone, in order to recall the cell x (the cell which has the x index) through its index and stimulate it. Otherwise if the cell x is a word cell, one can say a word whose phonemes are the characteristics of the auditory cell x, which will be excited in this way. A cell can be excited weakly or strongly. The excitation can be made to vary through cerebral processes that are conceptually mechanizable, which, in humans, are also voluntarily activated. A cell strongly excited through its index spontaneously emits (spontaneous emission) the information contained in its memory starting from the line which has the greatest power; this, for the cells of the auditory level, is almost always the line of characteristics, the last; then there are others, of the memory zone, each one with its own power: the power of the line is calculated adding up the persistence of the elements of the line. If the cell is excited through its characteristics, its index can be memorized and the line of the memory zone that has the greatest power will be

147

emitted. I note the difference between the lines of the memory zone and the lines of the characteristics of the cell. Let's imagine, for example to have the same set I of phoneme indexes memorized on a line of characteristics of the cell x, also memorized in a memory line of the cell y, let's say on the line u. If this set I 'passes' in the brain for example, because a word with these phonemes has been heard, the cell x will be excited, not the cell y which has their copy in the memory zone. Instead, if in the brain some of the indexes of the phoneme I circulate, they will excite the x cell very little because all the set is necessary to stimulate it. Another argument must be made for the y cell, if it were excited in the moment that part of I is circulating in the brain, this would make it emit all the content of its line u, that is all of I even if u is not the line of the greatest power. This case is about stimulated emissions which prevail and inhibit spontaneous ones of other lines of the memory cell, with greater power. The excitation of a cell takes place also in the presence of partial information contained in the line of its characteristics. In this case it is not a strong excitation but it can be added to a weak excitation from the cell obtained, for example, through the index. Always for example, at a visual level, if an object is looked for in an environment, the cell which contains the characteristics can be partially stimulated through its index in order that also a part of the image of that object seen in nature or only its high contracted lines, obtained through peripheral vision, increasing the excitation of the cell, to bring it to a highly excited state and therefore to the emission. A cell loses its excitation in a certain amount of time with a trend to be defined quantitatively. Also the cancellation of the element of the line of stimulation of the cell, which is certainly tied to their persistence, must be defined quantitatively. The cell can maintain the excitation through appropriate brain processes conceptually mechanizable. As far as the level of arousal of the brain processes is concerned, it is possible to say that the cell is strongly excited by impulses that come from the senses; less excited by impulses that come from memories. In a context of analogies there are differences between the cells of the visual system and those of the auditory system, due to their different functions, which are evident in humans. In humans the auditory sense substantially does not have the function of exploring and understanding the world but is intended for receiving the information communicated by another speaker and vice versa. The world is understood above all by sight. Certainly, a person recognises a cow or a goat by their voices but it is a residual task of the auditory sense, within a clear evolutionary trend, from which it emerges that it is intended for understanding spoken language. In humans the vocal apparatus is closely connected to the auditory system of the brain and permits the transmission of informative content of cerebral origin to another human. The visual system does not have an apparatus similar to the vocal one. The information between two brains takes place through the voice, not through the emission of images. The role of the auditory system in superior animals is different from humans and above all, within its limits, serves for exploring the environment. The information which the animal transmits through its vocal apparatus is very little as it does not have articulated language, nor a brain suitable for generating it. While there is sense in hypothesising that a strong excitation of an auditory cell, through its index produces the emission of its line of characteristics, does it make sense that a strong stimulation of a visual cell generates the emission of the configuration, which are the characteristics of the image? I would say no and, in agreement with this supposition, in the configuration the 'photograph' of the form is not conserved but rather the characteristics which make it possible to recognise it. However, it is possible that with visual memory, if the same, precise, identical figure is observed many times, the low contracted lines, those that are little elaborated, are reinforced and contain the information necessary to remember the 'photograph' of that figure. Furthermore the function of memorizing can be modified in order to obtain the memorization of the less elaborated contracted lines. Drawing a figure from memory is, anyway, a talent that few possess and is therefore something that has been given little importance in evolution, in my opinion exactly because communication between brains does not take place by means of images.

4. The formation of the object

Let us suppose that a phoneme cell is excited by a sound and simultaneously a cell of the visual system is excited by an image, isolated in central vision. The cell of the visual system memorizes the index of that of the auditory system in its memory zone and vice versa the cell of the auditory system memorizes the index of the visual system in its memory zone. In future, seeing the same image, the cell of the visual system will emit the information necessary for finding the index of the cell of the auditory system and stimulate it. In the simplest of cases the cell of the auditory system will emit the content of its line of characteristics: the phoneme, which will be easily transformed into sound. Vice versa, in the future, on hearing the sound, the cell of that phoneme will be excited and if this emits the information of the index of the cell of the visual system the consequence is the partial excitation of this image cell. Therefore if only a modest excitation of this cell comes from the eye, because it sees only a part of the figure, because it sees it with peripheral vision, therefore it perceives only the high contracted lines, it is enough to excite further all the cells, causing them to emit (usually) the index of the image cell. Therefore, even if the object is partially hidden, if it is immobile..., it can be isolated and recognised.

In humans , the formation of the object and language (which for the moment I have limited to phonemes) are closely linked. In superior animals I think that the role which non structured language has in humans about the formation of the object is carried out chiefly by the sense of smell. If the image of another animal and its smell are memorized together, the same process takes place as described above for the object and the phoneme. Afterwards the smell of the other animal will recall its image in the brain of the first animal. However, the comparison is not perfectly fitting because I think 1) in animals, also superior ones, smell is important in itself for recognising the object while sight serves above all to localize and reach it. This affirmation becomes more and more true as the evolutionary scale descends. Furthermore 2) the animals do not possess an articulated language and a similar structure is not to be found in the sense of smell. We can say that they distinguish smells much better than humans: for example elephants can distinguish around 8000.   3) Finally, a thing can be identified by a particular smell as is sometimes the same for sounds, for example the call of a hen. Instead, in humans the phoneme chosen for memorizing the image is conventional and remains connected to the image relative to an environmental state. In other words the animal, a cat for example, associates the shape of a mouse with its smell, the smell is a natural fact, independent from the will of the cat. Humans associate the shape of a mouse to an arbitrary sound: mouse, giari, topo,...which is used in the community. Even if I suppose that onomatopoeia has played an important role in the formation of language in primitive man. I have used words, not phonemes, as an example, to clarify the matter. Returning to phonemes, the same arbitrary phoneme pronounced a second, third,... time will recall the same visual cell which will be forced to memorize the environmental state superimposing it on what has already been memorized the previous times and the image will be refined through the normal methods known in the neuronal networks. For this a good teacher (human) will show his student (human) things he believes are similar, unconsciously trusting that both the teacher and the learner have the same kind of brain and see the same similarities in things, Instead a bad teacher can attribute the same name to things that are completely different. In this case, because of the function of the neuronal network, the memorized characteristics will be almost totally cancelled, except for the generation of homonyms. I have already spoken of these things in the part of the book about vision. The formation of an object without phoneme (or smell) is possible but I think I can exclude this way of proceeding. It doesn't seem to me to be the path chosen by nature: when the cat sees a mouse the second time, even before seeing it, the cat will have the same partly stimulated visual cell, recalled by the smell of the mouse and the memorization of the characteristics of the second mouse will happen in the same cell. Smell is very important for recognising, probably more than the image. Literature is full of stories of dogs that attacked their owners because they had an unfamiliar smell. The first case I know of is reported in an anecdote which cites Heraclitus of Ephesus (535- 475 BC) who was savaged by his dogs who didn't recognise him because, in order to cure an illness, he had immersed himself in fermenting manure. Perhaps when a newborn child memorizes his mother's face, it happens also through her smell. The object can be seen from different images but they are memorized with the same name. In fact if the angles are unchanged in the rotation that takes place on the perpendicular plane at the conjunction between the object and the eye, likewise the rotation that conceals the faces of the solid object holds up well, therefore it is not enough to rotate the solid object a few degrees in order to have different characteristics. In projecting software it is necessary to take into account how to register the different views of the object that are under the same name and also to be careful to distinguish this case from situations of

152

homonymies. Apart from homonymies, it is really possible to impose registration in different visual cells but with the same name the prospects that equal contracted lines have from a certain contracted line upwards. Incidentally I say that the "rotation" of an object is a transformation that recalls specific cells of the human visual system that give the perception of rotation, in other words what we see as rotation is in fact the stimulation of these cells as a result of a specific transformation of the environmental state.

The outline of a silhouette is usually the first to form because of movement and permits the isolation of the figure in central vision. Afterwards the internal contours are formed, from spots of colour within the principal object which are also brought into a vision which has a minor convergence than the previous one and from which the outlines are extracted. The outlines are usually closed, especially the external ones, unless the colour spot has a clear outline on one side and is blurred on the other, actually a very rare case. It could be a cloud. At cerebral level a figure always tends to close up, also expanding in length the lines where there is maximum gradient, also where the gradient no longer exists, through an increase in sensibility suitable for detecting the gradient,

Incidentally, I think one of the laws of Gestalt can explain this, one which states that objects have outlines that are closed and precise. It must be noted that this usually happens for solids while it is less true for clouds and water. I think that the closed outlines of solids come from the necessity to define the obstruction of a solid body in order to avoid it and not bump into it, getting hurt. Therefore the necessity of closed outlines comes from the necessity to localize the solid object more than the necessity to recognise it, for which complete outlines, also in my model, are desirable but not indispensable. The brain through evolution has learnt to recognise solids in order to not bump into them, because they block the light, it can be seen where they are in order to make the necessary adjustments. It is obvious that there are exceptions but they are rare and usually artificial and have not contributed to evolution: glass for example from which windows are made and which birds often crash against. The necessity to have precise outlines in an environment of enormous light variations and a modest variation of discharge is resolved with a differential operation and convergence of the visual system, with the inaccuracy that it entails. This is remedied with the information connected to the receptive field of the complex cells. I could be wrong, but the sensation of height that forms when the outlines are unstable which could preced their formation and do not require to be memorized with a name or smell, is perhaps a residue of the function of the primogenital cortical visual apparatus which was not made for recognising things but for locating them.

The process of expansion of the outlines is progressive and starts where there is the greatest gradient. It is a good thing to help the brain in this work and, in fact, the objects shown to small children have clear outlines and are produced in different colours that are not shaded. On asking a child to describe a solid form, he will say that normally solids have closed outlines, they are hard and heavy. In reality these are the sensations which they produce and which converge in a single memorization. I agree with Ernst Mach in defining the object as a bundle of sensations, and add that the object always seems to be the same, or similar if it is subject to a development towards the same end. Natural selection has created a nervous system for processing information so that objects are perceived as being identical, in the context in which humans evolve, in that they develop in order to provide the same benefit or harm to the living. Later, starting from this cerebral structure, humans proceed in generalizations and abstractions. A sub-object inside the silhouette forms in the same way and eventually it can be given a name. When the internal sub-objects are formed, they are related to each other by changes in the cerebral state. The most evident of these are eye movements. Eye movements connect two objects with a line that has a certain angulation measured with respect, for example, to the horizontal. Usually the object is seen in a certain position, for example, a face is always seen with the hair on top and the chin below, therefore, the angulation of the segment that connects ear and mouth in a profile is more or less constant because it assumes that the hair is on top. Then it is possible to anticipate a rotation of the object with respect to its usual position, in which case all the angles which form the lines which connect the sub-objects will be increased or decreased to the same extent. In neurophysiology the phenomenon has been studied and the time for recognising a rotated object has been measured. With the same method used for isolating internal objects, ulterior objects can be found inside them, as long as it is possible to scale them. The changes in the cerebral state can have a name, for example "above" can be the name of eye movement, "inside" the name of the transition from a minor to a major scale. The situation for articulated areas is identical to that of the sub-object. Changes in the cerebral state lead from the image of a man to that of a leg. The presence of these internal sub-objects may or may not be constant. Every time the object which includes them is presented they may be present or not, or at least, not all of them. Sometimes the presence of a sub-object can be decisive for recognising the object. Wording of the type "sometimes" can be put before the name of these sub-objects, if followed by the name of the sub-object and so on... In this way a sentence is formed which describes the object and its components. Therefore recognition will take place also through sub-objects, through their existence, their importance and the spatial relations between them. This can be described in a sentence where the sub-object and the changes in the cerebral state with which they are connected have names.

5. The formation of words

Let us suppose that in the auditory system of the brain there is no cell with memorizations in the line of characteristics. Obviously this does not concern the phoneme cells, each one of which is born with its own phoneme recorded and connected to a decoder. Let us then suppose that a word is pronounced which must be understood as a succession of syllables which, in their turn, are a succession of phonemes. To simplify the argument the syllable plane can be left out and the phonemes considered to be characteristics of the words. It is enough to take the precaution of considering the pauses between the words. The information of the indexes of its phonemes circulates in the brain and finds no coincidence because the lines of characteristics of the words are all empty. I hypothesize that in such a case a device intervenes, which is certainly an attentional device because it is connected to variations of sound which predispose an index cell i of the first plane (already the second, without the hypothesis of supplanting the syllables) of level U so that its line of characteristics can accept the registration of the indexes of the phonemes of the word pronounced. Let us suppose that the same word is repeated. This time there is coincidence between the information that circulates in the brain and that of the last line of the cell previously memorized. The word cell is not excited anymore by the device but through the line of characteristics and the persistence of the phonemes in this line is strengthened. A new word, never heard before, that is, it finds no correspondence in the line of characteristics of the other cells, activates the device which makes it follow the destiny seen for the first memorized word: it goes into an empty cell prepared with a procedure which is easily mechanized. In other words the device activates every time there is a word to be memorized that has not been heard before. There is a fundamental difference between words and syllables: every syllable has it phonemes (always those!), therefore when a syllable has been pronounced it is easy to find it in the memory or say that it is not there. Furthermore syllables have a phonetic structure that makes it possible to identify where they begin and where they end, words no. Usually, in almost all languages, words have a fixed part and a variable part and in order to be identified they need to be enclosed between two pauses (at least at the learning stage). The two pauses are necessary for memorizing all the phonemes in the line of characteristics of the word cell, even if the word does not have variable parts. Otherwise the word would be an unpredictable string of phonemes of length, variable every time, referring each time to a different cell and therefore not memorizable. Word cells must have a rigorously constant line of characteristics . Therefore, applying this reasoning, the words house and houses would occupy two different cells. This would not be an economic process, for example an irregular Italian verb forms dozens of different words "camminai, camminerei, camminassi, ... and for this the need arises, evident in all grammar books, to distinguish between the fixed part and the variable part of the word in order to reduce the necessity to only one cell for the fixed part and one for each of the variable parts to be associated to the fixed parts of other words. It is not simple to succeed in making a computer distinguish the fixed part of a word from the variable part with a human like method. " Bare" is the fixed part of bareback and barefoot but "can is not the fixed part of candle or canal. Grammar books, which are many and different from each other, more or less agree that the fixed part of a word defines its meaning and the variable part specifies it. This definition seems to explain the preceding example, in fact "bare" contains the meaning and "back" and "foot" give precision, while "can" does not contain the meaning of "candle" or "canal". Unfortunately the definition of meaning is vacuous, it is a metaphor because 2500 years have passed since Heraclitus of Ephesus considered for the first time what words should mean and also even if great intellectual energy has been spent since then, nobody has had, up to now, a clear or mechanizable idea of the concept it expresses. As it is indispensable, I too enter the arena and propose my definition, obviously operative. In my opinion the situation is similar to the formation of the image and the necessity of refining it, only now the roles are inverted. In the case that a phoneme (or a smell) was associated with an image cell every time that phoneme was pronounced (or the smell was perceived), the index of an image cell was recalled, always the same one, which memorized what the eye saw. In this way the image cell's memory was refined, with the typical processes of the neuronal network. If, instead, it is a certain image that recalls a specific word cell and simultaneously a word is pronounced whose phonemes deviate little from those in the line of characteristics of the cell, the phonemes which correspond will have their persistence increased, but not those which do not correspond and after a few times they can be eliminated with a threshold. Let us consider for example the word pencil which we think is memorized in the cell i of level U and we think that its image is memorized in the cell i of level V. On seeing the pencil the j cell will emit the i index which will stimulate the cell which contains in its line of characteristics the phoneme pencil. If at the same time the word pencil is pronounced, the power of all the phonemes will be increased but if during the stimulation of the i cell the word pencils is pronounced, only the phonemes "pencil" will have their power increased. Therefore hearing alternately pencils and pencil during the stimulation of the i cell leads to strengthening the whole group of phonemes "pencil" and to the possibility of cancelling the phoneme a or the phoneme of the line of characteristics of the i cell: It doesn't matter if the variable part of the line of characteristics is long or short, if it is within the word, at the beginning or the end, associating the word to the image, the power of the variable parts diminishes. It can be arranged for memorization of the variable parts to take place within another cell. I don't wish to avoid this argument but only to put it off, because now it seems possible to me to define operatively what is meant by the meaning of the word, going backwards, through the formation of its fixed parts and in accordance with the aforementioned grammatical definition: without an image that always recalls the same U cells, the fixed part of the word cannot be isolated, the image and the fixed part of the word are connected. Combining the definition which requires the fixed part of the word to be the part that conveys the meaning of it, the meaning emerges as the association of the word to the image and therefore sensorial data. This can be easily extended to the case of humans, one can speak of the meaning of words tied to smell, words tied to taste,.... perceptions of other senses which are not sight: it is enough that they are associated with a word, that is, their index is tied to the word index. The expression "meaning of the word" can be further generalized and a word can be defined by another word but there is the risk of metaphor. It will be seen that a word can also be defined by a phrase but the more we move away from the sensory world, the nearer we are to nonsense. However, a word can also have no sense, I would say asemantic, if this term didn't have a different linguistic meaning, in fact a word repeated always in the same way, separated well with pauses, can be learned because the first time automatic or voluntary excitation of a cell designed to accommodate it is envisaged. Given two asemantic words, presumably not very different, it is impossible to know what is their fixed part or if they are different words unless the variable part of their language has been studied. A method that does not seem human like to me. Differently from the word and transferring what has been reasoned about visual level, the image cannot be asemantic. Images in nature are never equal therefore automatism makes sense for learning an image"the first time" because it will never repeat itself identically, therefore a sound, a smell, something that recalls the same cell and permits the image to be precise is necessary. This has already been said but now we can conclude that the necessity of this association brings the impossibility of having an asemantic image.

Observing the physical world one notices that very many situations are formed by objects combined in different ways which cannot be defined by as many words, often situations must be defined through a series of different words, each one designating an object and in this way a phrase is formed. The phrase can be memorized in a memory cell which contains in its lines of characteristics indexes of words. It should be noted that the line of characteristics of the phrase cell is composed of the indexes of the word cells, and therefore in order to form the phrase string words must be formed. Furthermore the phrase, above all in the learning phase, must have a beginning and an end marked by two pauses. I would also like to point out that the phrase cells can contain in their lines of characteristics indexes of some words, repeated, preceded and followed by a pause, it may not be possible to define such words as phrases in a grammatical sense. Identically the phrases must be formed in order to be the index of the period cell. Etc...., etc... The indexes of the inferior cells constitute the line of characteristics of the superior cells if and only if their characteristics are included with two temporal pauses. More than a very high vertical structure which concerns a whole long text I would see many lower pyramids along the text. Probably there is no sense in going higher than the period cell. The phrase cells and, even more, the period cells need to be maintained in a stimulated state for a long time in order that the line of characteristics can take form.

6. Level A. Actuator cells

Muscles are devices that make the eye move from one point to another of the scene, they can stop, focus,... These muscles and biological apparatus are commanded by electrical impulses, molecules, which go round the brain and in the artificial brain they can be considered to be actuators, mechanistic transposition of the muscles or also, by extension, other cerebral apparatus. They are controlled by impulses. The level of the actuators is identical to the auditory level and its cells, they have the structure of fig. 68. There are also cells that are similar to those of phonemes, each one of which is connected to its apparatus and carries out an elementary or atomic operation. For example there is a cell that is stimulated when the eye turns to the right, another that is stimulated when the focal distance increases. How many actuators there are and consequently how many are the cells applied to them depends on how the artificial brain is constructed but their number is finite and not very great. If the eye is made to look upwards it is because the specific actuator has received a command formed by impulses. The cell, let's say k, of the actuator level which has in its lines of characteristics impulses for making the eye look up, is excited. Inversely when that cell k is excited through its index the cell it emits the impulses which make the eye turn up. In parallel with the auditory level. The stimulation of the phoneme cell "r" comes through the work of a sound that arrives from the ear which is elaborated in the decoder and stimulates its line of characteristics; inversely if the stimulation of this cell happens through its index, the cell through a procedure which is conceptually possible, perhaps by inverting the decoding process, forces the vocal chords to vibrate, as the eardrum vibrates when it receives the sound "r". As a consequence the speaker utters the sound "r". It is also true that the eardrum and the vocal chords are distinct organs but the conceptual validity of the argument does not change, it is only a question of constructive opportunity. The process of memorizing is always the same: if the eye is made to turn upwards, one of the actuator cells, for example the k cell, is excited. If at the same time the word "up" is pronounced, the word cell of level U is excited, which has the addresses of the phonemes of "up" in the line of

161

characteristics, let's say, of the h cell. The h cell memorizes the k index in the memory zone and simultaneously the k cell memorizes the h index in its memory zone. Following this the word that was heard, the word "up", the excitation of the h cell will recall the k cell which is in the actuator level and make the eye turn; while, in the case of the eye turning up to follow a raised finger, the k cell will be excited which will recall the h cell and the word "up" will be emitted. Then there are other cells, in analogy with the word cells of the auditory system, which have the indexes of the actuator cells in the line of characteristics ,or others, superior which have as characteristics the indexes of the latter, in analogy with the phrase cells. I will call the series of actuator cells level A.

7. The literal memory

I think that in the auditory system there are two types of memory: one which we will call pyramidal memory and a second which I will call literal memory, the argument of this paragraph. Let us suppose to have memorized the words of the Italian vocabulary, let's say in 5000 cells. In these conditions (without interruptions) we recite: The glory of he who moves everything through the universe penetrates... Saying "The" I excite the cells that have these phonemes in the line of characteristics, it is the same saying "glory", "of",... these word cells have in their indexes, which I suppose have respectively the values of 12, 23,75, 132, etc... The cell number 12, has it line of the characteristic excited by the phonemes "The", is excited by the pronounced word, but its excitation vanishes after a little time, to be specified with quantitative considerations, which I suppose are sufficient for memorizing the indexes of the words "glory" and "of" but not the rest of the phrase. When "glory" is pronounced the cell which has the phonemes of "glory" in the line of characteristics is excited and the cell will memorize the indexes of the words "of" and "he"; then the excitation of "glory" will fall away and will not be capable of memorization anymore. Pronouncing the word "of", the cell which has this characteristic will be excited and will memorize the indexes of "he" and "who", etc,... Essentially each excited cell memorizes the indexes of the words ahead. If a word cell X is strongly excited by the indexes of the phoneme cells, which it has in its line of characteristics, it becomes capable of memorizing for a certain period of time. Since in that time other word cells are stimulated, the X cell memorizes their indexes in a line of memorization. If the reading is repeated in order to learn a poem by heart, the programme controls and finds that in the memory zone of the cell "The" there is a line with the indexes of the same words which are being pronounced now and strengthens the power of the registration. If we want to remember a passage, when the registrations have been memorized, pronouncing only the word "The" the emission of a more powerful line of memorization of the cell may occur but if "The glory" is pronounced, the cell of the word "The" of the index 12 is excited and the cell of the word "glory" of index 23 too, but most important of all is that the index of the word "glory" will be the stimulation which will make the line of memory of the cell "The" containing "glory of" emit. Therefore the cell 23 of the word "glory", if excited strongly, emits stimulated by the indexes which come from the cell "The" for which it emits "of who" or better still, the indexes 75 and 132. From now on instead of speaking of indexes I will use words because this gives a more immediate result. It should be noted that "The" has emitted "glory of", the cell "glory" has emitted "of who" and therefore the cell "of" is excited by two emissions originating from the brain cells not from the decoder activated by a speaker. The excitations of the decoder are powerful, those of the brain less, however, if "The" and "glory" are pronounced very rapidly the two "of" emitted (glory OF, OF who!) interest this

163

cell summing up their effects and taking it to a sufficient level of excitation and to the emission stimulated by its line which contains "he who", etc... Therefore having said two words in order, the memory of the text starts. It doesn't matter if the two words are the first or if they are to be found at any point of the memorized passage, what is important is that they are in order and they start the memory of the words that come after. All this does not have a quantitative value: it is an example. The word memorized in the line of a cell could be 4, as 3 cellular emissions of the same word could be needed to take the cell to a sufficient level of excitation. In fig. 69 there is an example of the function of a stimulated emission. The cells are 4. In the first line of the table there are their indexes. The last is the line of characteristics which contains the phonemes of the word that belong to that cell. In the second line there are the memories of the poem memorized in every cell, together with many others, indicated by the dots on the third line. To simplify the discourse, in the second line I have put the names of the cells while the indexes are memorized in them. Therefore instead of writing in the first cell "glory of" it would be correct to write 23, 75, if we want to be even more precise with their persistence. Under the table, in the first line there are the words spoken by an external speaker, each one of which is enough to strongly excite the cell. In the second line there is the emission of cell 12, the one of the word "The", that is "glory of". Cell 23 is excited twice: from the word "glory" pronounced and from the index number 23, the first time strongly because it is a signal that comes from hearing and the second time more weakly because it is the emission of cell 12. The two excitations sum up and a very strong excitation comes from them. The cell 75 "of" is excited by the emissions of 12 and cell 23, they are weak stimulations but if summed up they are sufficient to make it emit in its turn. As there is the index of the cell 132 "he" in the memory of cell 23, the emission of the line of cell 132 which contains the index of "he" will be stimulated. It is the

164

same for cell 132 "he", excited by the emissions of cells 23 and 75 and their emission is stimulated by "who" present in cell 75 which make "who all" emit. At this point the process takes place and is maintained. I would like to point out again the two functions which each word has (or better the index of its cell has, which, however, contains the same information). In this development, for example "he" emitted by cell 23 excites cell 132 and stimulates the emission of the part of memory "he who" of cell 75. The word "he" emitted by cell 75 in the part of memory also excites cell 132 and makes it able to emit, naturally in a regime of stimulated emissions.

12	23	75	132	indexes
glory of	of he	he who	who everything	memory zone
......	......	......	......	memory zone
......	......	......	......	memory zone
......	......	......	......	memory zone
the	glory	of	he	charact. zone

the	glory			pronounced word
	glory	of		emission from cell 12
		of	he	emission from cell 23
			he	emission from cell 75
strong	very strong	sufficient	sufficient	cell excitation

Fig. 69

In this type of memory it is necessary that the cell remains excited, that is, it is able to memorize, while the successive cells are excited. Therefore it doesn't seem to me that literal memory can concern the phrase cells and even less the period cells, unless it is expected to keep them stimulated with a voluntary act and a device suitable for

165

this purpose. However it could concern the phoneme cells, more than the word cells for which I have developed the example. The literal memory is substantially asemantic, it could be formed by asemantic words.

8. The pyramidal memory

The name pyramidal memory suggests how it is formed even in a long text, with phonemes as a base, then syllables, then words, then phrases,... up to the last cell, at the top of the pyramid. Proof is necessary but I believe that the pyramids are not very high. Furthermore I think that how the pyramidal memory is formed, by the phrase plane, whose cells have the indexes of the word cells as characteristics, does not happen as for a word cell, whose stimulation is (also) the work of an automatic attentional device. The phrase cell, for example, must be maintained in a stimulated state for a relatively long time and therefore a wilful act is necessary. Keeping a cell stimulated voluntarily is a big leap in quality· up to now I have only spoken of automatism and I think that the existence of this possibility and the device that carries it out contribute more than any other apparatus, to explain the difference between the thoughts of animals and those of humans. A difference already detected by Descartes. In order to memorize the line of characteristics of a phrase it is necessary to voluntarily keep the cell stimulated while the words which substitute the phrase are pronounced and the beginning and end of the phrase must have clear temporal pauses, superior to those between the words. During the formation of the phrase, in pyramidal memory, the words must already be formed, because the characteristics of the phrase cell are the indexes of the words but these can be pronounced with a minimal pause between them. They are stimulated by the succession of the phonemes that coincide with

166

the one that has been memorized, after all it happens to humans too, who, when knowing a language, we can follow the speaker who doesn't need to articulate the words. What has been said for phrases also applies to period cells and superiors but also for the word cells, which can be maintained in a stimulated state voluntarily. This happens, for example, when a new language is studied at school. For words, however, also automatic stimulation applies. As an example, a phrase cell of the i index is stimulated and in its line of characteristics it memorizes the indexes of the words "Poi che crescendo viene" (then with growth it comes), and simultaneously another phrase cell of the j index is stimulated, which contains in its line of characteristics the title of the poem already memorized "Canto notturno di un pastore errante dell'Asia" (Night song of a wandering shepherd from Asia). The cells memorize their respective indexes and during the reading of this wonderful poem the phrase in question recalls the title. The advantage over literal memory is that it is possible to recall the title of the poem without having to read it all to reach the title, whatever it is, at the end. The title mustn't be placed within the poem with literal memory because then it would be an indistinguishable part of the poem during its recital. It is possible to take some phrases, or also some words from the poem and let the title be memorized in the pyramidal memory. In the same way phrases or sentences can be included in cells, also other information such as: this is a beautiful part of the poem, here the author recalls the thoughts of a certain philosopher,... information that is generally fragmented but in many pyramids which have as a base short pieces of the text. It is appropriate that there is at least one reference to a common cell, which permits all of them to be connected. This can take place, for example, by memorizing a lot of information relative to the text in the lines of memory of the same cell j, which has, for example, the indexes of the words of the title for characteristics. The index of the phrase cell which has as the line of characteristics the title of the poem, makes it possible to obtain the information which belongs to the poem; the name of the author, the date when it was composed, the collection it is part of... Everyone organizes the pyramidal memory as they wish but it is a voluntary effort.

9. Relations between the pyramidal memory and the literal memory.

There is little that is new in this paragraph, it is dedicated to clarifications and specifications.
The passage "Odi greggi belar, muggire armenti" (hear flocks bleat, herds bellow) possesses clear semantics due to the two phrases and it could be checked in the environment. In literal memory the passage is subject to an environmental control through a device I will speak about in the next paragraph. From the control it can turn out to be true or false and therefore draw the consequences of the case. For example, as a square is a geometrical figure with four equal sides and angles, it is possible to check if the drawing in front of us is a square or not. Having established this our thoughts can proceed to decisions or other definitions. Pyramidal memory instead takes us in other directions which are not the control of the phrase. In fact in a passage in literal memory there are parts which recall memories which have nothing to do with the phrase we are checking; we could talk about drought, great heat, the scorching Sun referring to a meteorological map of Piedmont but in pyramidal memory these words make us think of Saudi Arabia, as a phrase cell can be stimulated also by a part of the phrase, that is, also from the indexes of a few words that are in the line of characteristics. Precision is not necessary. In my opinion this is the mechanization of a particular kind of intuition which is fundamental for thought as Poincaré rightly argued. Intuition is good but, of course, it has to be checked.

I would like to point out the analogy, which is not equality, between pyramidal memory and the configuration of the visual level. The pyramid U is formed by cells, each of which has the capacity to memorize. The visual configuration also has a pyramidal form but represents the characteristics of only one cell which has only one memory zone. The cell of the upper level U is chosen casually, while containing the indexes of the layer immediately below; the element of the upper layer of level V has values which derive from the operations on two elements near the lower level and is connected spatially with them. Furthermore the element of the visual cell does not have the capacity to memorize, it is simply an element of the characteristics of a cell. Furthermore rising up in the layers of the visual level there is a generalization of the information because the form loses non-essential particulars. None of this happens in the planes of the auditory level.

In the visual level a distinction has been made between vision and the capacity to recognise, which, among other things, connects U and V and makes it possible to define the semantics. Also in the auditory system the possibility of recognition exists: the phonemes can be recognised and also for the auditory system it is necessary to distinguish between semantics and the perception of sound. I think that the phrase, sentence and also word cells have little to do with the perception of sound. They have semantic ends. The perception of sound is due to the phoneme cells and to the attentional mechanism that they trigger which place the living in relation to the environment. Perception derives from this relationship.

In the visual system the phonemes find a parallel with the elements of the first contracted line, the one connected to the eye, which finds the edges and their position from the signal which arrives from the retina. However, while the words, at least in their fixed part, are always formed by the same phonemes, it is not so for images because the angles, the main characteristics of the form, are changeable for

169

the same real figure, unless it is the same object, for example, the same face, always seen from the front, or even better the same geometrical figure, or a photograph. In this case memorization takes place also in the contracted lines of the first layer, the one connected to the neurophysiological apparatus, which, starting from the image as it is projected on the retina, obtains its characteristics. It is, however, a very exceptional case. In fact it is not important if memorization takes place in the first layer of the visual cell, which would allow the backward process from which to obtain the image as perceived. This is because the visual system is not needed for communication. There were men with super powers who projected an image on a screen with their eyes only in the comics I read as a child. Nature has not followed this evolutionary path. It is true that some people (very few) are able to draw a face without having it in front of them. The vision of the image through the memory of it in the visual system is therefore uncertain. However I think that amongst the cells of the human visual system there is the analogous of literal memory. Let us consider a person who walks along a street and looks where he is going. I have already pointed out that the contracted line remains constant compared to the variations of the figures. This implies that the memorization of the route takes place through a distinct succession of different configurations, each one of which represents the characteristics of a visual cell. If i is a stimulated visual cell, immediately after it the cell j will be stimulated, then k, then n. In the line of memorization of the cell i the indexes of j and k will be memorized; in the cell j the indexes k and n will be memorized,... Naturally the length of the chain must be defined with quantitative reasoning. Repeating the same route several times the images which follow each other will be learnt and with them will be learnt the turnings, which are the commands to the actuators, for example the legs, to follow the path. Therefore although it is not possible to visualize in memory "like in a film", the

170

route is memorized. The distinct succession of cells would seem to implicate vision in a series of jerks while everyone of us while walking sees the landscape unfolding continuously. It should be remembered that in the visual system there are two branches, one linked to recognition and one to localization, vision is part of the latter, configuration the former. It is also true that the two functions overlap widely because they make use largely of the same neurophysiological support but they must be kept conceptually apart. The movement which develops as continuous derives from the stimulation of particular cells of the visual system, whose existence manifests itself in the operation of the complex cells of the retina which are sensitive to movement in a direction. The succession of images are made to seem continuous by particular cells and memorized in linear succession which makes memorization seem to be a way of making the path appear clearly. Instead it is possible, without modifying the principles of literal memory, to have in the memory zone of the visual cell r two lines s and t from which two different chains of literal memory start. A sort of crossroads. With different effects and purposes, the auditory perception reaches the cerebral stimulation of the phoneme cells, from a signal that arrives from the ear. The stimulation of these cells in the brain produces a reverse process in the auditory system, from the brain to the exterior, that is, the emission of the sound which had stimulated them. The sound is reproduced by the vocal apparatus, through the vibrations of the vocal chords, not through the vibrations of the eardrum in the ear., but this is a constructive detail, like those which permit the sound to be self-perceived even if nothing is said, if the signal which originates in the brain is present, it should make the vocal chords vibrate.

The phonemes in words, but even more in syllables, are constant and are conserved in memory, they are not like the elements of the last layer of the visual system, which are variable and become lost. Also without the automatic attentional device, which stimulates the empty word cell or the analogous device which stimulates the phrase cells and the sentence cells on a voluntary basis, a word could be formed by pure literal memory, between phoneme cells without the necessity of a word cell, in fact, phonemes are precise, if a group of them is repeated they could be memorized only in literal memory. It doesn't seem to me that in humans things go in this way. I think that literal memory is above all to be found in words, pyramidal memory in phrases and sentences. I think that the control device, of which I will speak in the following paragraph, stimulates the phonemes starting from words.

I would like to point out that a sequence in literal memory, let's say of words, can be elongated, recovering some words at the end and repeating them. In the same way words can be added at the beginning of a previously memorized sequence. It is enough to repeat a few times the words that are to be put at the beginning of the sequence with the initial words. A phrase can also be inserted in a point of the text that has been learned in literal memory. It is enough to say some words of the text that come before this point, the inserted phrase and then some of the words that follow the point. The previous link of stimulated emission between the words before and after the point are weakened, while the text before the point where the inserted phrase started and after the end of the inserted phrase are strengthened. They are all hypothesis which will be refined with tests and more tests.

10. The control device

The role of the control device is to verify the connection of a phrase to the physical world or also to memories in the brain. For now I will limit the argument to the physical world. The control device allows the implication, conditioning it to the certainty of control. Therefore this implication has an intrinsically doubtful and probabilistic nature.

1) It can make the sentence flow stop temporarily, for example, to allow the execution of the commands contained in a word, like the one that makes the eyes move. Then it can resume the flow of the sentence.

2) Furthermore it allows the commands contained in the words to act on themselves and these actions are prioritized. In particular:

a) It can change the order in which the words of the sentence are verified or the order in which the commands contained in the words are carried out.

b) It manages the "brackets" which means that the words contained in them are acted on before those that are outside the brackets.

c) It allows the substitution of a word in the sentence, for example, with another word or phrase.

d) Finally the control device is capable of a property similar to that of distributing logic between the words of a sentence, the words, brackets, substitutions and distributive properties recall constructions of symbolic logic but are not to be understood in that sense or at least not precisely

3) When the device is forced, as can happen in a sentence for learning, for example, to control a word instead of another, violating the order of the word contained in the sentence, it emits impulses which, if they are registered in a word, when this is pronounced, they emit them again, the control device will repeat the operation and change the order of the words in the new sentence. This is the most important hypothesis which I think cannot be modified with tests, which instead can improve the function of point 2).

An example of the function of the control device can be verified if there is a table in the environment where it is possible to proceed, for example, to lay it. In this sense the control device manages the implication. There is a question "is there a table?", therefore the word table emits the index of the image cell of the table, which remains weakly stimulated. If it is necessary to look and see if there is a table, it is probably necessary to go and look for it with a complex procedure which I will leave for the moment. We think that if the table is there, it is in front of our eyes, that the light is correct, that the eyes are focused, etc..., otherwise the visual scene is empty or there is another object. If the table is there, the image cell of the table will emit the index of the word cell "table". The control device, having ascertained that the table exists because the word table has been emitted with reference to the image of the table which is in the environment and which has stimulated its index, gives rise to the appropriate implication. On the contrary, if the table were not there, its visual cell would not be stimulated (if not weakly from the recall in the brain of the word table) and it would not emit the index of the word table. It should be said, however, that recognition is not always very certain, principally that which is topological, as I could see using vision programmes. It is possible to improve but there will never be absolute certainty, for this reason the implication has a probabilistic nature. A further example of how the control device works can come from eye movement on an object formed by more objects, each one of which has its name but they are related spatially and are in order, that is, one above the other or one inside the other or one to the left of the other,... The same control can take place with different phrases. The reason why one object is controlled before another, in general, is because an object

174

has greater visibility than another, even if the least visible object is usually the important one. If I say that the chair is to the right of the table, the eye checks the table before the chair because it is more evident than the chair, because it can be found more easily in the environment, or rather it is the reference for finding the chair more easily. The speaker in formulating the phrase, keeps this in mind. For the moment I limit myself to the control of the phrase and not to its formation. The phrase to be controlled in its environment is: "the light is over the table". As I have said the verb to be in a first approximation can be ignored, and also the articles can be ignored. The word "over" has in itself the need for a starting point, it has an implicit question connected to it, it is as if it were written "over (where?)" Only after this question has been resolved does the eye look up. In order to explain how the control of a phrase that contains the word "over" takes place one could say that the control device first checks the noun after the word over, then it acts on over and then checks if the remaining noun is in the right place. Over has two functions: it defines the order of the controls of the phrase and makes the eye look up. For example in the phrase "the light is over the table" which is simplified to "light over table" the control device arranges the words as table >over (eyes look up)>light and controls them in this order. The same succession takes place for the phrase "over the table is the light", that is "over table light" acted out as table >over(eyes look up)>light. The word over is acted out only after the presence of the table has been verified, the most visible object in the environment and only then one can think that the eye looks up, checking that the light is vertically over the table. It seems to me that the expressions "on the right of", "on the left of", etc... and the ones which contain the word "below" can be treated in the same way: Always as an example I could study the function of the control device in relation to the conjunction "and". The "and" has the function of maintaining the brain in the state acquired from the preceding phrase or word. I have already said that a precise definition of phrase does not exist. I propose for the moment to call a phrase a succession of words with a verb, therefore the sentence would be composed of at least two phrases. A sentence is: there is a table and over it there is a light; in fact there are two phrases which I will close between brackets, one that comes before "and" and one that comes after: (there is a table) and (over it there is a light). The phrases are checked one at a time, in this case in the order in which they are found. With the first phrase the attention is fixed on the table and the brain keeps it because of the conjunction; the second phrase begins with "over" and the brain finds that the starting point is defined with the attention maintained on the table and causes the eye to rotate towards the light. In fact in the second phrase the question "where", always connected to "over" requires a pronoun or noun or an indication of place. If it happens that a pronoun is required, it can be left as understood in Italian. I understand how the sentence is formed but it is a topic that I have not yet touched on. It would be different if the wording were: "there is the table over a light". There would be just one phrase, "over" would be noted immediately and would take as a starting point the following word "a light" and then look for the table. The sentence "there is a table, over it there is a light", that is (there is a table), (over it there is a light) does not have "and" to keep the starting point in mind. The sentence is not very natural, few people would construct it in this way. The sentence "there is a table and there is a light over it" seen as (there is a table) and (there is a light over it), does not create problems of interpretation: "over" is checked and has "table" as a reference point. Continuing with similar examples does not make sense, indeed it can be misleading because it should not be a programmer who specifies the functions that the word "over" have in the English language and in the language of the computer: the machine must learn them by itself by forcing the operation of the control device and other actuators. If I say to a child that the light is over the table, in order to find the light and I know that he understands the meaning of the words table and light, I tell him: look for the table, because it is easier that the child will see it before he sees the light. In this way the word table is controlled first and the control device emits the impulses that indicate the variation in order of the controls. When the child finds it, I make gestures which bring the child's eyes to go up, repeating the word over so also this undergoes an anticipation of the control and finally he sees the light. During the control, every word of the phrase is stimulated and then memorized. The words light, over and table memorize the various impulses that run in the brain while the phrase is controlled but only the word over maintains the memory of the commands that have produced variations in the controls because in a similar phrase table could be substituted with mountain and light with Moon. Furthermore the words table and light can also be found in other phrases where other impulses are memorized. However, the information that the word over must be controlled first is not forgotten and it activates only after it has been fixed in a place, that is the fixation of an object which, given its variability, is forgotten. Furthermore over must have a starting point and an arrival point which are often only implied. Over can also have different meanings but they are few and the same procedure as for synonyms can be followed. I say "the lesson is over" this over, is understood as a synonym of finished. To that end, however, it is necessary to understand a phrase that is far from its physical context. Incidentally I will say that classical grammar would see the word over as a preposition, adverb and subordinate conjunction in the three cases mentioned above. Just to highlight the impossibility of parsing and the consequent failure of translations based on parsing. It is precisely the underlying idea, due to Chomsky, that is wrong. The grammar of natural language described as terminal alphabet, non terminal alphabet and production rules is a chimera: nobody could ever have precise rules of production in natural language. It is not precise, it is ambiguous and at times contradictory, it is enough to observe how we reason. Such a method would function well for writing and analysing an artificial language such as programming languages and, in fact, those who do this work are in debt to Chomsky. However, I agree with Chomsky, perhaps with the first Chomsky, on generative grammar, which for me comes from ergative language, from the description of the situation at the start, distinct in agent and patient and from a verb that indicates what is the transformation that the agent performs on the patient. When this transformation takes place, how long it lasts, with what probability it will take place etc... are refinements The verb to be does not indicate a transformation but is the description of a compound object.

I would also like to point out that, as opposed to the part dedicated to vision, I have not tried out these theories of mine on the computer, therefore they can contain many errors: Trying and trying again will bring about modifications and improvements to the functions of the control device but not the essential ideas of the mechanization of structured language which are 1) the control device and 2) the hypothesis that every actuator and also the control device, while carrying out a function, produce impulses and that, on receiving these impulses, carry out the same function.

The device controls the implication, the parentheses and, implicitly, the negation. I suppose, but for the purposes of this text it is not of interest to prove it, that from these logical operations all the others can be obtained. Allowed but not granted that the device produces formal logic, natural language is often ambiguous and contradictory; also the way people reason and their language is often not very logical, much less axiomatic. Furthermore the connection between the world and the brain is uncertain, therefore implications or predictions are doubtful and a formally correct description like logic can only find a modest and limited application in my way of understanding the brain function which is to ensure a prediction, inevitably uncertain. In fact sensible people have little faith in long arguments and always check their conclusions experimentally. Which is none other than the teaching of Galileo. Logic has a value in itself as a branch of mathematics or philosophy but my opinion of it as a basis for thinking is very far from that of Leibniz and his calculemus.

11. Understanding the written text

Perfecting the prediction of the development of a physical situation takes place first by controlling a phrase that refers to it. However, it is possible to think of replacing the physical situation with memories, expressed in literal form or in visual memory from which the same information can be derived as it would be derived from the physical situation. Obviously in this way the risk of incoherency is great, post galilean physics is precisely the refusal of the application of this method if not as a hypothetical theory that must be followed by an accurate check of the physical situation. Galileo's teaching is completely disregarded in the human sciences and is beginning to be disregarded in physics too by many who are not resigned to the observation of Erwing Schroedinger. According to him: "in an honest search for truth we must resign ourselves to ignorance for an indefinite time", and they take shortcuts. Not to mention what happens in many High Schools and Universities where, instead of teaching the students how to conduct experiments, computer simulations are preferred. Having said this and that I am not interested in correcting bad habits, the problem arises of how to find the information of interest in the brain. For example I have the following sentence in my literal memory: Giacomo Leopardi was born in Recanati on the 29th June 1798. I propose to answer the question "Where was Leopardi born?" The machine can easily find Leopard and born, any search engine could do it, therefore the problem is partially resolved but the question "Where?" remains. One could think that a place name is always preceded by "in" while the date is preceded by the article "the" as is generally found in solicitors' deeds and in the sentence above. Therefore could the computer be programmed for finding the word after the preposition "in"? This is not always true because the sentence "Leopardi was born in Recanati in June" makes sense but the machine, programmed in this way, at the question: where was Leopardi born? would reply "in June". Articles and prepositions are absolutely not discriminating in order to answer the question "where?". It entails understanding the text in order to have a satisfactory answer which, according to me, is impossible without semantics. The machine must know that Recanati is a town, a place and therefore can be associated with the question "where?". This implies that the machine has previous knowledge. The word "where" has the indexes of the words place, town, country and similar placed in its memory and in addition the indexes of the cell A which activate every time the senses reach a place. Also Recanati certainly has the index of the word town in its memory, which is probably the memorization with the highest power and probably the first to be emitted when the word "Recanati" is recalled, this means that "where" emits in turn, by stimulated emission the word "town". It would be absurd to think that the word "where" has in its memory all the towns of the world and the word Recanati starts

180

the stimulated emission from these memorizations. I think, even if it will take a lot of evidence, that the repeated excitations of the word "where" brings it to emit successively all its memorizations until it finds correspondence in "Recanati", which must be excited repeatedly and the correspondence provokes the stimulated emission of a line of its memory. If "where", after it has emitted all that is in its memory cells, does not provoke the stimulated emission of the word "Recanati", the words that it has emitted could be excited, for example the word "town" could be stimulated with the attempt to provoke with spontaneous emissions the spontaneous emission of "Recanati", They are mechanizable procedures. However, it is indispensable that the words "city" or "town" or something similar are memorized in "Recanati". If a child does not know that Recanati is a town, reading the sentence in question he cannot understand where Leopardi was born. The question "who/which" functions similarly, the machine needs to know that Galileo was a person, that is the words person, man, are memorized in the cell called Galileo but also indexes of images...., likewise the word "who/which" should have in its memory: men, animal,... and proceed as before. It is therefore necessary that in every word there are many memorizations. The phrase cell memorizes in the same way as the word cell. For example saying "The dialogue on the world's maximum systems" stimulates the phrase cell which has memorized in its various memory cells, indexes of various excerpts of texts designed to trigger a literal memory process, as follows: it was written that Galileo compared the astronomical systems of Copernicus and Ptolemy. The Ptolemaic system was taken up by Saint Thomas and supported by the Catholic Church. The book is written in the form of a dialogue, the Ptolemaic system and the case of the Church was upheld by a poor man named Simplicio who was laughed at,...

Appendix I – Complements

1. Learning by differences

While the mechanization of language is superior to my possibilities and energy, I have succeeded in creating an automatic procedure that helps to define an object through various topological perceptions, connected by changes in brain states and eye movements in order to discriminate between objects that are topologically similar and tend to be confused. This starts from is the revelation of the differences between topologically similar objects. Already the Ancient Greeks discussed if learning took place through similarity or differences. The two methods are not mutually exclusive, while the real problem is defining the similarity to which an identical development of the situation must correspond. Two apples of different qualities appear to be similar because evolution has formed the brain to bring together different environmental states into similar brain states. This applied initially to odours then, further on in evolution, the sense of sight. Similarity is a result of evolution to satisfy primary needs, instead the discriminating difference can be relative to one purpose as it can be inessential for another. This much can be seen in human vision where eye movements vary on the scene based on the quality of what one wants to detect. For example the picture on the wall of a church is observed in one way if one wonders "do the angels have trumpets?" and in another way if the question is "are the angels richly dressed?", we owe this discovery to Yarbus. These changes of state, these perceptions, these eye movements,... are associated with words: this much implies that the scene of the picture will never be fully described by a series of words, at least in usual language and in cases that are not abstract, such as geometric figures. Nothing changes if in the picture there is only one object, an angel for example. An object, if it is not a mathematical construction, can never be fully described by a phrase. The phrase brings to light that which the speaker thinks is important. Having said that I proposed to myself to construct again a phrase for recognising the forms Q and O for reading purposes. Obviously the difference is in the tail at the bottom and its detection can be mechanized. Let us suppose to have memorized the forms O and Q, amongst various other forms very different from these two such as T,X,B, etc. If I show them to the computer and launch programmes of recognition for the drawing of a Q, it will probably reply that the form in question has the name "capital q" with a probability of 80% while for "capital o" it will give a probability of 65% for which, given the small percentage difference, it will not be sure and will search for the difference between the two forms, finding it in the tail at the bottom. If the first time the form Q is presented to the machine, in order to recognise it, the isolated protrusion could be recalled with the name "tail", previously memorized. If the visual space is divided into two areas, one called bottom and the other top, with the word "bottom" the position of the tail can be detected. It would be much better to have a video camera that moves, that can be zoomed. However, if the elements that constitute the tail have ordinates lower than a certain value of the protrusion of the Q, it is associated with the name "tail" and the name "bottom". The tail is a particular which the O does not have but the Q yes. Keeping in mind that the reference is the form of the O, that is in the memory and whose name is known, the words tail and bottom can be associated with the O together with the word "with", a brain state that expresses the presence of a particular in perception, absent from the memorized form. The first two names concern two perceptions, the third and fourth are the revelation of brain processes. The phrase could be "O with tail bottom=Q". Probably it is useless that I remark that in the previous phrase the symbols Q and O are not to be considered as forms but as their names. The symbol "=" is for indicating that the phrase that follows is the definition of Q. This symbol could be substituted by the word "to be". Such a phrase is emitted by the machine because both the images and the variations of cerebral state stimulate cells that recall names. Naturally the phrase can be memorized and used in future for distinguishing the form Q from the form O. Identically the phrase "Q without tail bottom=O" can be derived, demonstrating the new form O to the machine, having Q in memory. I guess that it should be possible to arrive at this second phrase with rules of logic, inverting the letters and changing "with" to "without". However, it seems less immediate because the application of this inversion rule which changes with to without could also change bottom to top. I have always been diffident towards purely logical-syntactic constructs. Learning by differences is very important for forming a phrase. However, it is not very important that the protrusion has a name, it is isolated in the differential learning process, scaled and stimulated in a visual cell whose index will be memorized in the phrase, as are the commands contained in the word "bottom" and in general, those which generate changes of state can belong to level A and therefore be nameless.

2. Some examples

In fig. 70 the current figure, a C, has been compared with an A with the result of having very few correspondances, in particular almost none inside. I remember that the dark grey (green for those who see the figure on the site) indicates that the corners are not connectable. In fig. 72 there is a comparison between a form G current figure, of which the machine does not know the name, with a residual figure called C-------, of which the machine knows the name and has memorized the characteristics. The comparison was made with an old programme, still in dos, with the resolution of that period. The characterisitics of the current form are schematized on the upper side of the "rectangle" at the top, on the left, which should be considered the development of a perimeter of the form G. Those of the residual form are on the bottom side. The 6 small circles above the rectangle must be counted from 0 to 6 and find correspondence with the 5 small circles on the perimeter of the current figure G, where 0 is the highest small circle and corresponds with the 6th small circle. The figure is counted in a clockwise direction. It can be seen that links are missing between the sides of the rectangle, between the small circle number 2 and that of number 3, in correspondence with the element which a person would say is distinctive between C and G.

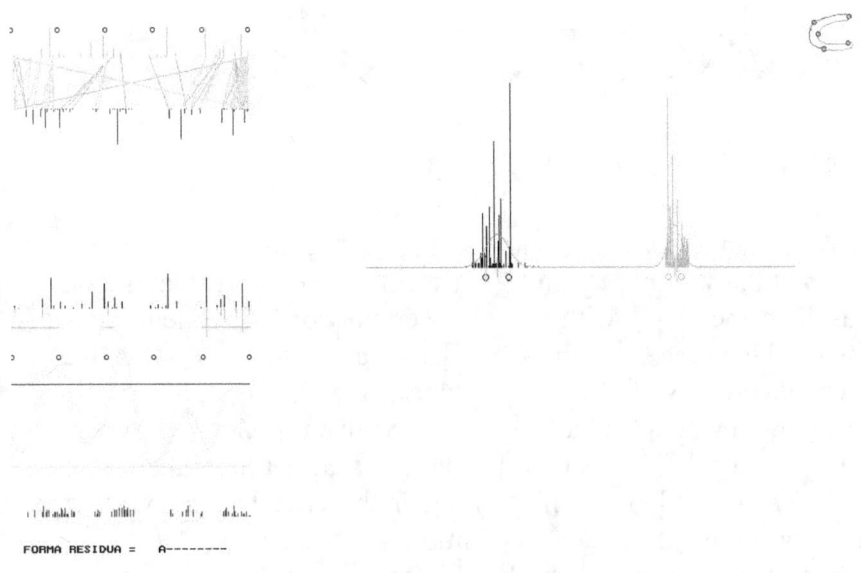

Fig. 70

In fig. 72 instead, the links are shown between the current figure G, the same as before, and another form with the name G------, which could be said to be a G with a different shape. The difference is detected and accepted and the links between the line of characteristics of the current figure and those of the residual one are

185

sufficient. POT indicates the level of certainty with which the machine assigns the name C----- or G----- to the current G shape.

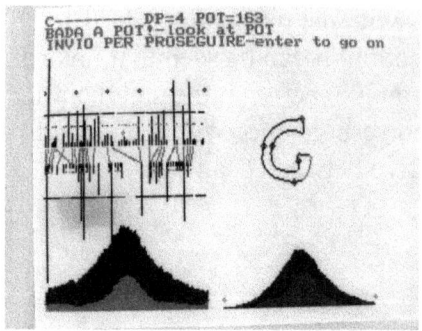
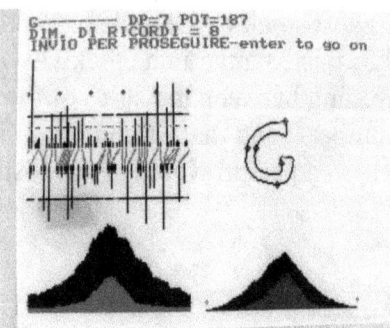

Fig. 71   Fig. 72

Let's remember that we are in the phase of topological recognition or, better still, by similarity. In fig. 71 the machine asserts that the shape has the name C-----, with a level of certainty of 163 while in fig. 72 the machine writes that the same shape has the name G----- with a level of certainty of 187. Undoubtedly 187>163 therefore a rough recognition would lead to the conclusion that it is G-----. However, relatively the difference between the two shapes is not great: 163/187=0.87, 87% of similarity and in this case the system activates the procedure of syntactic recognition. Between A and C the difference is enormous already with topological recognition and other analysis are not necessary.

In the figs. 73 and 74 there are the various shapes of the forms C and G. Teaching the computer using a single shape, it is not confused between C and G, even without syntactic recognition, much less with other letters of the alphabet that do not resemble these.

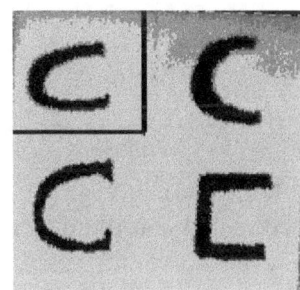

Fig. 73

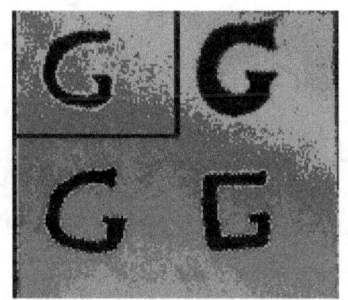

Fig. 74

A reasoned bibliography

For more detailed information the texts below can be consulted:

F. G. Tricomi, Lezioni di analisi Matematica (Mathematical analysis lessons) part II, Padua and by the same author Esercizi e complementi di analisi matematica (Exercises and complements of mathematical analysis) part II, Padua. They are university texts. There are explanations on two variable functions, on their representation, on gradients,...

P. Caldirola, G. Casati, F. Tealdi, Corso di fisica (Physics course) vol. I, II, III, Milan. They are High School texts. They introduce vector operations, field concepts, photometric and electrical units of measurement.

L.Maffei. L. Mecacci, La visione dalla neurofisiologia alla psicologia (Vision from neurophysiology to psychology), Milan. A great deal of information on the neurophysiology of the visual system is clearly explained.

D.Hubel, Occhio, Cervello, Visione (Eye, Brain, Vision), Bologna. The neurophysiology of the visual system is treated in depth. It is a fundamental text.

R. Pierantono, L'occhio e l'idea, fisiologia e storia della visione (The eye and the idea, the physiology and history of vision), Turin: It completes and, at times, shows in perspective different topics covered in the two preceding books.

R. L. Gregory, Occhio e cervello (The eye and the brain), Milan. The author directs his attention to the evolution of the visual system, to comparative physiology, moreover, in the volume there is a collection of optical illusions, many of which I also deal with and explain in a different way.

A. Rosenfeld, A. C. Kak, Digital picture processing, New York, San Francisco, London. It teaches how to process images on the computer. The text is dated 1976 but it is still valid.

M.Nitzberg, D. Mumford, T. Shiota, Filtering, Segmentation and Depth, Berlin. It teaches how to process images on the computer.

A. Plebe, Riconoscimento linguistico e visivo, teoria e tecniche (Linguistic and visual recognition, theories and techniques), Palermo. It is a text for those who want to start extracting edges, recognising shapes and also recognising sounds on a computer.

P. Scaruffi, La fabbrica del pensiero (The factory of thought), Turin. It is a book from 1994, it presents the history of artificial intelligence up to that date. Anyone who reads this book will see how my approach to the argument is different.

S. Russel, P. Norvig, Artificial intelligence: A Modern Approach, London. It also presents a brief history of the studies made on artificial intelligence. I appreciate the efforts of this author but whoever reads this book will realise that my way of addressing the argument is completely different.

In my book I have mentioned various scholars: F. Atteanave, C. Enroth-Cugell and J. G. Robson, R. H. S. Carpenter and C. Blakemore, N. Chomsky,...

References can be found in the bibliography of the above mentioned texts for tracing their original works; furthermore they put the reader, cultured but not specialized, in the condition to understand them.

Alphabetical Index

Contents